THE BENT-HANDLED
SNOWSHOVEL

First edition, May 2022
Copyright © 2022 Judy King
All rights reserved.

Published by Penciled In
5319 Barrenda Avenue
Atascadero, CA 93422
penciledin.com

ISBN-13:   978-1-939502-47-6

Editing, book layout and cover design
by Benjamin Daniel Lawless

THE BENT-HANDLED SNOW SHOVEL

BY
JUDY KING

CONTENTS

1   Page One

4   In Print

10   Happy Ever After

21   All in a Day's Work

32   Games People Play

39   Nutty Neighbors

44   Family Traditions

48   Home Repairs

53   Humor appropriate and inappropriate

69   Water Wonder Land

77   Driving

88   Just one of those days

101 Travel

106 Gift Giving

112 Surgery

120 Housekeeping and Home Appliances

131 Shopping

137 The Family with Children

142 DIET (Just another Four Letter Word)

152 Furry Family Friends

158 Single and Seventy

163 Last page

165 About the Author

THE BENT-HANDLED
SNOWSHOVEL

PAGE ONE

I believe attitudes are delivered in a laundry basket. You have an opportunity to sort through and pick the ones that best suit you and toss the rest into the lost sock drawer. You avoid the negative influences in this world by digging deep into that basket and finding that positive attitude that helps you see things in a new way. Often this new positive attitude walks hand and hand with a keener sense of humor and that's a really good thing.

The day I was born the doctor held me up by my feet and slapped my behind and that's when I am pretty sure my serious bone fell out. I have led a pretty good life without a serious bone in my body. This gave me an opportunity to grow an enormous funny bone in its place. I see the humor in just about everything in life. Sometimes that's a good thing and at times it can be a real embarrassment but it always leaves us with a story that travels from generation to generation.

Most families have these little treasures tucked away in their family archives and after a few years the classics become epic and you might just be privy to some original, never performed, real-life antics which leave everyone in gut wrenching laughter. In these pages I am sharing some of the stories that have kept our family entertained for years.

If you do not have a sense of humor I suggest you put this little book back on the shelf but if you decide to read it, I hope it brings a smile to your face and brightens your day.

I would like to thank my children for putting up with me over the years. You have given me more joy than you could ever imagine. I love you all.

I dedicate this book to my late husband Dale. It was quite a ride. I was blessed to have traveled this road with you. If you were here today, you would have many more stories to add to the mix.
I carry you in my heart forever.
Thanks for the good times.

IN PRINT

My grandmother wrote a short column for a small hometown newspaper in the late thirties and early forties. These stories were mostly about who had a birthday and who attended. They were very charming tidbits of information. I still have faded copies tucked away in a scrapbook and it amazes me how simple times were and how little it took to entertain with the written word.

A few years ago I decided to subscribe to the local paper and have it delivered directly to my house. What a convenience. I would cancel it when I went up north during the summer months and I would continue delivery in the fall when I got home. One day I discovered that my subscription could be transferred to the lake for the summer season and I was quite excited about that. I informed the distribution department to no longer stop delivery at home in the summer as I would like it delivered to the cabin during those months.

"No problem," they said. "Happy to do it."

I really was happy getting my paper at the lake until I got a call from my home neighbors telling me I was also getting the paper delivered at home. What? After several calls the home delivery was reduced to just the Sunday Paper and I told the neighbors to have at it.

As the summer progressed the lake delivery was inconsistent at best. *Ugh!* When the summer ended and I returned home I called again to cancel all deliveries forever, as if that were possible. I was done with getting the paper at both places but the home Sunday paper just kept coming.

After several calls about this I was told that my message was received and for me to stop calling.

I told them I would be delighted to stop calling and if they wanted to keep delivering the Sunday Paper I felt no obligation to pay for it.

The free delivery went on for a couple of years. During this time a friend of mine who had a subscription was not getting her Sunday paper so she called and asked if she could have mine since I got mine on a regular basis and didn't even have a subscription. I would have thought that would have been some kind of red flag. By now everyone in town had heard my story and eventually it must have gotten to the right people as one day it just stopped. It is pretty scary to think that this is the generation that will be tending to me in my old age.

Have you ever subscribed to a magazine? What a convenience. I paid my money up front and I was good to go. I filled out the proper form and mailed it in with my $20. This was my guarantee that for the next 3 years this informative periodical would magically appear in my mailbox. Well, don't bet on it.

For the first few months things went along as planned but then I discovered the word was out and every magazine printed in the world was sending me letters singing the praises of their print. I guess the publisher of my chosen magazine had a big, big mouth. Six months into this agreement I got a notice that my subscription was about to expire. WHAT? Now I am writing dates on my calendar and making phone calls. By participating in this crazy subscriber's world I am now a preferred customer and I may be eligible to receive $1000 a week for life if I just jumped through a few hoops. So for the next year I would paste stickers on forms to be mailed by certain dates and spend a fortune on stamps and numerous trips to the post office. I am pretty sure this time I will win this money for life but if, by chance, I should not there is a bright side: I have been given the opportunity to subscribe to some pretty amazing magazines for half price.

I really don't trust all those automated systems that are designed to save you time and money. My kids shop online. That sounds a little risky to me. When I hand out money with one hand I expect my purchased item to be on its way to my other hand. Why on earth would one want to order something by looking at a photo? Do you have any idea how many really bad photos of me are floating around? I would hate to think anyone would want to meet me after seeing one of those.

My daughters twisted my arm until I caved. I ordered a couple of bras. To my surprise they were delivered to my door the very next day. Wow, maybe those girls were right after all. Then I found out they did not send the right bras. I double checked the order, and these were not the bras I ordered.

No problem, I will just fill out the return form and send them back but there was no return form. I called my daughter and she said I had to print my own label but because I was going to her house the next week I could return the bras at a store near her and they would take care of everything. Whew!

Two weeks later I dragged the bras to that store only to find out they could not do it stating something about a third party. "No problem," my daughter said. Her husband could take the bras to work with him and print a label and send them on their way.

So now my bras are in the hands of my

son-in-law and on the way to his office. In the meantime a late charge of $30 was added to my new credit card because it had taken so long to return the bras. After an hour or so I finally got to talk to a real person and got the whole thing settled.

I thanked her for her help and told her to have a good life and I assured her that this would most likely be the last time she would ever hear from me. To stay true to my word I have my daughter or a friend do all my online shopping which makes everyone happy including my son-in-law.

HAPPY EVER AFTER

I met Dale C. King in high school. He was adorable. It was the 50s and he was all the 50s had to offer. Slicked back hair, a pack of Marlboros rolled up in his shirt sleeve, tight fitting pants, dimples you could put your fingers in. I couldn't wait for my parents to meet him. I'll never forget that "deer in the head lights" expression when I introduced him to them. Who cares? I'm keeping him.

I graduated high school at age 17, turned 18 in October and became Mrs. Dale King in January. I know my parents had college plans for me but that just wasn't going to happen. No, I had met the guy of my dreams and nothing was going to stop us. We were on our way to the adventure of our life. How cool was this? No curfew, no flashing porch lights. This was the happiest day of my life, bar none. I remember mother asking me how we would live. I replied, "why, on love of course."

That first upstairs apartment was a dream for us. There were three doors at the top of the stairs. One was the bedroom, one the bathroom and one the living room with an attached kitchen which had one cupboard with a curtain in place of a door. Every night we would lock our living room and bathroom and go into our little bedroom locking the door behind us. Of course if I had to use the bathroom in the night I made Dale get up and stand outside the door just in case someone came up those stairs. We were in marriage heaven.

This poor guy didn't know what he was in for. I could bake rolls, pies, cookies, and so on. I could live on this stuff forever but I figured now that I had a "husband" I had to up my game. My first glance into the supermarket meat case I knew I was in over my head. I didn't know there were so many animal parts. I picked out a limb that was in my price range, took it home and fried it. To this day I don't know what cut of meat it was but I do know you couldn't cut it with a saber saw.

I was never much for sewing although I did make a skirt in high school. As I proudly modeled it at the style show my mother was the only one who was under the bleachers. She said she had dropped her lipstick. Sure! When my husband broke the zipper in his work pants, I did the only thing a good wife could do. I sewed them shut. If he couldn't hold it until lunch time I was sure his boss would let him run home where I could cut him loose and stitch him shut again. It was only a couple of blocks. He said he would rather his bladder burst.

I learned a lot those first months of marriage. I discovered if you left cinnamon rolls in a covered container for a month they turned into a big furry animal, and after a week of using the same coffee grounds the coffee had a nasty, slimy green color.

We had friends visit us who had a baby and left a used cloth diaper behind. I was sure they would want it back so I saved it. Did you know the toxic fumes from a dirty cloth diaper confined in a brown paper bag for days on end can wipe out a small village?

Me neither. My mother thought a rat had died in the apartment.

"I know mom, isn't it terrible? It's that dirty diaper my friend left."

She took the bag in two fingers and with watering eyes and a pinched-off nose buried it in the back yard. I don't think any of this surprised her since she had just downed a cup of green coffee. I also learned that goldfish can jump from their bowl, slide under the sofa and not be discovered for weeks. Maybe I should have dusted more often.

We took our mattress everywhere. We didn't own a car so when friends invited us over it was understood the mattress came along. We would haul that lump of fluff down the stairs and strap it onto the top of our friend's car. No need to drive us home after a late night card game. We just stayed over. No extra room, no problem. Our landlord found this quite entertaining. You know, newlyweds and all.

Our furniture was early attic. There was a lot of preferred seating. In other words you probably preferred not to sit on the end of the sofa with the broken springs. Our apartment was right next to the railroad tracks. Our hand-me-down bed was on castors so when the train passed through in the middle of the night, the bed would travel across the wood floors. What a ride.

We spent our first six months in that location and I will never forget it. Best six months of my life. Years later, after I lost my husband, I parked my car behind that old house and looked up at that old apartment. I laughed and I cried.

FIRST MOVE

After that first six months of wedded bliss we decided it was time to upgrade. Our rent had been $50 a month with utilities included. We were lucky to find an apartment on the same side of town with a rent of $55 for the winter months which included utilities, but in the summer months we only paid $45. When your weekly income is $50 a week this is a big step-up.

This was what I called a shotgun

apartment. It started with a bedroom at one end, leading into a living area, then into a small isle kitchen and ending with a bathroom the size of a closet. We were in heaven.

Every now and then we might have to search under the car seats for change to buy a can of tuna, but we never regretted the move.

I killed my first layer cake in that apartment. Just couldn't get that icing to stick so I sure enough stabbed it to death. I think my husband Dale pretty much slept with one eye open after that.

Things started looking up when Dale got a new job making $100 a week. What should we do with all that money? Maybe it was time to start a family. So we decided to rent a house.

MOVE #2

We found a house a few blocks away and moved right in. I loved being pregnant. Huge maternity tops made it possible to consume dozens upon dozens of donuts and still feel good about myself until I gained 50 pounds and delivered a 7 pound baby. We named him Randy.

Now this baby thing was all new to us. I didn't know babies took up so much of your time and on the third day home from the hospital I clutched the front of my husbands shirt and while sobbing blurted out, "I will be stuck here with this baby forever and I will never be able to go roller skating again."

That's when my husband reminded me I had never roller skated in my life and all would be fine, and it was.

We purchased a stroller and with baby in tow I wore the wheels right off that thing. Freedom at last!

MOVE #3

We decided the house was a bit much and to save a little money we started looking for a cheaper place to live. With baby in tow we found an apartment on the other side of town.

This apartment had previously been the living quarters for nurses. There was a tunnel in the basement leading to what had been a hospital. Spooky!

Except for the kitchen and bath all of the other rooms were the same. We drew straws to see which room would be what and settled in. We were there about a year. Our moving schedule was getting pretty predictable.

With baby two on the way, we packed our belongings and with the encouragement of our parents decided it was time to join the world of real grownups and purchase our first home.

MOVE #4

The realtor could not wait to show us this little diamond in the rough. More like a diamond in an abyss. Fencing encircled the yard which was hidden by yards and yards of grape vines. Seems this place had been empty for a few years. It had been overrun by a pack of wild black cats which was almost a deal breaker for Dale. We assumed the sink propped up against the wall was the remains of a kitchen. The single register in the middle of the floor puffed out clouds of gray matter on a regular basis. Yeah, the furnace works.

We were in love with the place, so for $7000 we entered the world of home ownership. We did some upgrades and with my father's vision we had a pretty cute little place.

Another diet of donuts and a 50 pound weight gain gave us a 6 pound 5 ounce baby girl. We named her Robbin. Life was about to get interesting.

MOVE #5

Now, with two young children we were feeling pretty cramped in our little nest. Not willing to part with our first house we decided to rent it out. We purchased a house in the same neighborhood and moved once again.

This place didn't feel like home so when the renters moved we headed back to our first house. We were getting pretty good at this moving thing but we still needed more space so... let the remodeling begin!

We removed walls and added rooms, which in turn gave us the space we needed for one more baby. Same diet, same weight gain and "it's a girl," 5 pounds 13 ounces!" We named her Jeana.

After 19 years we had that place looking good and it was time to move to the other side of town.

MOVE #6

Wow, this place was huge. I had always wanted one of those big old houses. Probably read far too many gothic romances. Hmm, I don't recall these books mentioning the upkeep and heat bills... you know, bare facts.

We did love that big old barn even if we nearly froze. There was plenty of room for all of us and the big winding stairway was just what I had always dreamed of.

Sometimes bigger isn't always better. The two older kids were on the verge of moving out and we found ourselves longing for a smaller, cozy abode. Seems the "I want to live in a castle "era had passed. Load 'em up and move them out.

MOVE #7

Found a smaller house in a great neighborhood and have been here over 30 years. Of course we spent years removing walls and remodeling but that's just what we do. This little place has seen us through the "empty nest era" and into the "age of grandparents."

Now that I am alone I feel blessed to live in such an amazing neighborhood and a house just my size. Of course nothing is chiseled in stone. Life is always an adventure for me and after 35 years here I made the biggest life change ever.

Who would have thought that I would not only leave this home but I would leave town?

ALL IN A DAY'S WORK

After being married for a year I applied for my first job: Motherhood. I applied for this position with absolutely no training and no experience. *Bingo*, within nine months I had the job. The fact I could punch in while wearing my pajamas was a perk I could live with.

For job security, I had two children by the time I was 23. When these two started school I cut my hours from 24 a day to 19 and took on a second position in a grocery store. Sure did miss those pajama perks so I applied for my old hours back and had a third baby.

When my baby started school I thought, what now? I was too old to have any more children so I got the bright idea to start an in-home daycare. I could have had every kid in town. One mother said she felt good to leave the kids with someone who opened the door in her pajamas. Sort of like grandmas house. I liked the kids old enough to entertain me and that they did. There are a million stories I could tell about those years. I would make them lunch and sit them on the front porch just to terrorize the mailman.

I went into shock one day: I looked out and they were gone. It seems the high school band had marched by and the kids all marched off with it. *Yikes!* I found them down about a block away and from then on, no more porch lunches.

The kids were great and when I needed a few weeks off for some surgery my neighbor took them. After three days she was on a heart monitor and by the end of the week she had left town. Monday morning here they were at my door. One said he had been on a hunger strike for the past week and would I please take them back? They promised to be good and would help take care of me, and they did.

Eventually they grew up and I outgrew the baby-sitting era. Time to get back to the outside world and that brought me to the best job ever.

It was a hot summer day and a group of us were hanging out at a nearby lake. That's where I met Bob. Somewhere in conversation Bob offered me a job at his newly purchased vending company and I accepted. Looking back I am pretty sure the consumption of adult beverages had something to do with my answer. It turned out to be the best job ever. I agreed to show up Monday morning and I did. I was the first woman to work there and I was twice as old as the other three guys including Bob, the boss. I'm pretty sure they were looking for a younger gal but this is where immaturity really pays off. Now this little business was just getting off the ground and was housed in a dilapidated yellow pole barn with only enough room to house two dry-cleaner reject vans.

Along with vending, Bob had started an office coffee service. He had five accounts and needed someone to take this part of the business on and see where it could go. That sounded like a lot of fun and I loved a challenge. I was told I would be coming in early to count money before I hit the road, and if anyone tried to break into the warehouse I was to shoot them with the pistol that was in a holster under the desk. I laughed and the first thing I did was check it out and sure enough there was my protector. I knew I had to pull my weight with these younger guys. Who knew these guys would be friends for life?

As the years passed the business became very successful and each time another guy was hired I found another lifetime friend. It's been years since I have worked there and I still keep in touch with all of them. My boss and his family have become part of my family. In later years my son would work there and was privy to all of the crazy stories from days gone by. I love those guys and hope they will all be there when they carry me away. I don't even care if they are old and have to use the lift truck.

This job allowed me to travel several counties in one of the company vans. Every time I entered an office I felt sorry for the poor office employee who had to sit at a desk and stare at the back of someone's head all day. Nope, not me, I could play my music loud and travel unknown dirt roads, meet new people and drink in the scenery. What a job.

One day I got a memo that it was the driver's responsibility to keep their vehicle washed. I thought, now how hard could that be? I had never used a car wash before so I figured my first experience should be enlightening. I chose a do-it-yourself facility in a town far away from where I worked, you know, just in case I made a fool out of myself. What were the chances of that? It was a cold and windy day, my friend, when I pulled into the icy booth. Not being one to read instructions I held the wand nonchalantly in one hand and fed my quarters into the slot with the other. IF I had read the instructions they would have said, "Make sure pressure lock is in OFF position until ready to wash vehicle." Seems mine was in the ON position. That wand flew out of my hand, bounced off the wall, hit me in the head, broke my glasses and all the time drenching me with ice cold water.

I managed to get hold of the beast and hanging on for dear life I skated myself out the door and did a few twirls in the parking lot. I wrestled that thing until my money was spent and it lost its power. I located my broken glasses and wove them into my frozen hair, which sat upon my frozen head with a big frozen bump on top. At the end of the day my boss took one look at my rumpled appearance and broken glasses and assumed I had been robbed. As I retold my story there wasn't a dry eye in the place. They still get a good laugh recalling that day. Needless to say from then on the van washing ritual was left to someone else.

Rule number one: always lock your van and hook your keys unto your belt. Rule number two: always use your emergency brake when parking on a hill. No one told me rule number two may not work if the hill is covered with ice. The last thing you want to hear from a receptionist as you walk into an office is, "Miss, I think your van is moving." WHAT? I went skating down the drive practically ripping off my pants trying to unhook my keys from my belt and managed to fling myself into the driver's seat and steer that beast to safety.

All eyes were on me as I reentered the building. "That was nothing" I said, "I began my morning upside down in a trash barrel at a gas station retrieving my glasses that flew off my face when I ran head first into a gas pump while trying to exit the van because I thought it was going to blow up." Turned out the hissing sound I was running from was nothing more than a box sitting on top of an open aerosol can. Did I mention it was a can of foam cleaner?

On a slow day I could be found riding with one of the guys helping him out with his route. We would visit factories and other facilities making sure all of the vending machines were properly filled. This is a whole book in and of itself. We all wore key locks on our belt and you cannot imagine the things I got stuck on that lock besides keys. I once got a huge wire pastry rack filled with pastries hooked on my belt. It took two of us dancing around the parking lot to free me. I think every employee in the factory was looking out the windows that day. Nice we could entertain them.

Our vans were equipped with only a driver's seat and a wall separating the front of the van from the back. When I helped out on short trips someone had to crawl into the back. Not me, I have a thing about small places. Even the shelves stocked with candy could not lure me back there. One momentous day I somehow convinced my boss to get back there. He could peer through the slit at the top of the wall and gave me directions. I was laughing and joking around when I heard him yell, "STOP SIGN, STOP SIGN!" I slammed on my brakes and I could hear candy bars flying for a good minute. Next question: should I let him out at the next stop or just cut my losses and make a run for it. As I opened the door, there he sat covered with candy and chips. He was not a happy camper but in time we had some good laughs over the whole incident.

As my part of the business grew from five accounts to over three hundred, covering seven different counties... I needed help. The office was taking up most of my time and I eventually hired two gals to go on the road. Now this is not a job for everyone. The girls had to be responsible for their route, load their own van and carry a tool box for minor repairs. They had to get along with all kinds of people and know just how much product was needed at each stop, and they had to roll with these truck drivers. I did the hiring because if the guys had a vote they wanted every little cutie that walked in the door even if they didn't have the brains to pound sand in a rat hole. There is something to be said about being older and wiser.

I was starting to form a personal attachment to my old blue company van when it all came to an abrupt halt. It was a balmy spring day and I was singing my lungs out along with my favorite country song when the unthinkable happened. Out of nowhere came a deer. I hit him head on and he flew up in the air, looked me in the eye, spun around on the pavement and walked off. I managed to drive to a nearby store where they towed my dear blue friend away and brought me a replacement. I'll bet there are some good stories going around that junk yard.

Now I love deer. They are cute with those big brown eyes and they look so innocent. I have always said it was not the deer's fault that man came along and built roads and highways right through their forests, so when I hit the first deer I felt really bad and with a big van no less. After the next two car/deer incidents I was whistling a much different tune.

Deer two and three actually ran into me. I'm thinking they either had a death wish or they were just plain stupid. Then one day I figured it out. Both times I was driving one of those little compact cars. I think the deer lined up on the side of the road and the conversation went something like this:

DEER ONE: "Here she comes again, what do you think?"

DEER TWO: "Is it a real car or just one of those little tin toys?"

DEER THREE: "I don't know, but I think we can take her." Wrong.

Reporting a deer/car accident is a real hoot. The first time the officer asked me which direction the deer was coming from, you know, east to west or north to south etc. Then he took out a little ruler with deer cut outs on it and preceded to pencil in the shape of the deer. When he lifted the ruler there were these little deer leaping across the page. What is this? Kindergarten? I wanted to burst out laughing but figured not the time or place.

When I hit my third deer I had to travel a few miles to report it. Now I'm thinking there has to be an unseen reason for this. Maybe there will be a nice single officer at the end of my journey and who knows? Not to be. The officer I met was about 12. He escorted me into the parking lot to see if there was any evidence of the collision. Seems the poor deer has to leave some DNA behind before it can be called a real accident. These guys crack me up. I am driving a much larger car now and hopefully these creatures will take heed and not be so reckless with their lives. Not holding my breath.

GAMES PEOPLE PLAY

I grew up with the athletic ability of a gnat. I spent a lot of time working my way to the back of the line so I didn't have to bat that baseball, and if I did happen to hit the ball my chances of getting to first base were pretty slim.

I almost always had the spot across the volleyball net from the girl who could kill a lion with her bare hands. Being hit by one of her balls could render you unconscious for days.

I crawled around on the floor a lot.

I never learned to swim until I was an adult so I spent a lot of time on shore.

If you ever saw me wearing a blue ribbon you can rest assured it was on loan from my very athletic friend who usually felt sorry for me on field day.

Now I look back at my inabilities and have a good laugh. What a wimp.

I have learned to love baseball — I said love, not play. At age 70 I swam across my lake and took up biking. Isn't life just a kick in the pants?

I never have learned the ins and outs of football but I do know when my grandsons names come blaring over the loud speaker, that's my cue to stand up and yell, "That's my grandson." That's his cue to point to someone else.

These days most of my sports involve a deck of cards or a board. I play for fun so if you are one of those guys who will be quoting Hoyle (whoever he is) every ten seconds you probably don't want me as a partner. Lucky I still have all of my ten fingers just in case I have to add more than two figures. I have found that there is more to playing cards than one would think. First you have to master the art of the shuffle. I have seen people flip those laminated squares in a million different ways and deal them out without missing a beat. When it is my turn to shuffle I usually end up under the table retrieving those slippery little guys and after I have composed myself and the cards have been dealt some one usually says," who got too many cards? Looks like I am short one. MISDEAL.

Next it is time to choose a partner and it's school sports all over again. No one is going to want you on their team. Lucky for you there is usually someone who will take pity on you and say they are only there to have fun and winning isn't everything.

They lie.

Most of my partners were born with a deck of cards in their hands and a killer instinct to win at all cost. There are some card games where you don't have a partner. You play your hand alone with no chance of dragging anyone down with you. I like that idea. What could possibly go wrong? I disappoint myself everyday. I just may have found my game.

No one told me about the unsolicited feedback. Here come the card police: "Why on earth did you play that jack? I would have never bet on that hand. You had a hand like that and you bid nothing?"

You hope this humiliation will soon be over. From here on out you ditch your cards before anyone can see them and say, "gee I just cant get a break tonight." even if you had the best hand you will ever have

I asked a friend a few years back if he thought I could play cards at the casino and he said, "yes, but don't play at my table."

It appears that BINGO is a big hit with game players. A friend of mine and I were invited to attend one of these events. We were told we might win some money. Seems they go all of the time. This should be fun. Neither one of us had a clue.

We got in line to purchase our sheets (I did say purchase and therein lies the money you hope to recoup). Then you get your dobbers or dabbers or what ever. No cards and corn here. Let the fun begin.

We watch as people start lining up little "good luck" charms and chanting "good luck" phrases and we were hoping we would not have to eat a raw chicken. What. The. Heck?

The caller starts reading off numbers and the lady in the pink flowered dress starts yelling, "What? Was that a B or a G?" Then the guy, with the bib overalls, yells to the lady, "Shut up, we can't hear." Someone else hollers BINGO and half a dozen follow up with, "Gee, I only needed one more number, so close." The lady in the tight t-shirt is getting madder and redder in the face each time someone else wins and we figure she is going to blow at any minute. Where did they say the exits were?

Snacks are there to be purchased but our friends smuggle in all kinds of treats and tell us to help ourselves. We are sure we will be arrested by the BINGO police as we nonchalantly ruffle through the bulging bag. At one time I yelled BINGO but really didn't have it. How embarrassing!

I looked at my friend and the pressure to hold back was too much. As we burst out in laughter we were told that BINGO players take this game very seriously and we could get kicked out. None of that helped and the hysteria over took us. Thankfully the evening was nearly over and everyone collected their little BINGO trolls. We were informed of another game the next week.

We declined.

Table games can be a lot of fun. Just leave

your luck to the roll of the dice. Of course you do run the risk of sitting by the guy with no self esteem and winning this game is the only way he can face the world. The coward within me overrides my sense of achievement and I spend the rest of the game trying to lose so this guy can feel good about himself.

What can I say? I just don't have that killer instinct.

Now there is always bowling. Throw a ball and knock over a bunch of pins. How hard could that be? Believe me: those pins are a lot farther apart than they look. Being the diehard that I am I joined a bowling league. Oh, the pressure to keep up with the pack!

Now if I could just bowl in my back yard and mail in my score I think I would have done a lot better. Twice I accidentally dropped the ball behind me. I had to hand it to the team for keeping a straight face.

During the short time I did belong to this league I had the honor of attending a state bowling tournament. It was in St. Louis, Missouri. Oh, this trip totally made up for my embarrassing moments. These gals were crazy. We walked the river front. The captain let us steer a riverboat down the mighty Mississippi and we got to see the beautiful Clydesdales. I liked the little gray one until someone pointed out he was a donkey. We stood under the arch, ate tons of good food and didn't sleep for three days. When my husband picked me up from the bus my feet were swollen and I had lost my voice. He asked me how I had bowled. Bowling? Oh yes, pretty good I guess...

Oh, to what extents we go just to entertain ourselves! Some go to the casino expecting to get rich. The last time I went I lost $10 and thought, gee, I could have gone to the movies. I guess the internet has a multitude of games to play but I am sure I would probably punch the wrong button and end up losing the farm. It takes a good mind to master your way through that system.

Guess I will stick to what I know best: being a spectator and cheering on the crowd and getting a few laughs along the way.

NUTTY NEIGHBORS

For many years I have known it is true
that a family of squirrels had elected a crew
to build a home in the pine tree high,
out of the reach of the predictor's eye.
Large enough to house the young and old,
and strong enough to weather the cold.

They started around the first of May,
scurrying about most of the day,
gathering sticks and twins and twine,
and just about anything else they could find.

They never gave up until the job was done,
no time for silliness and no time for fun.
At the end of summer it seemed to me
they had built quite a home in the top of that tree.
That was years ago but with annual repair
generations of squirrels have found refuge there.
So at the end of the day as the world shuts its eye,
I think of that family up high in the sky.

Over the years I have had a few incidents with our little beady-eyed, fluffy-tailed friends.

There was that *death by Jell-O* incident that the family will never let me forget. It was a holiday gathering and I had made festive-finger-Jell-O treats for the grandchildren. With no room in the refrigerator I balanced the tray on the back porch railing. It was a cold winter day and that seemed like the perfect place. Imagine my surprise when a few hours later I went to retrieve the pan but it was not there. As I peered over the railing there was the pan, the Jell-O and a dead squirrel. I think he must have really liked Jell-O or he had a death wish.

I went to check on my good friends house while she was away and you can only imagine the shock when I turned the key and opened the door to discover a squirrel flying up the stairway right towards me. I screamed and he made a u-turn into the main floor of the house making all kinds of clucking noises which summoned all of his outside friends to gather in the nearby tree to cluck back. I stopped screaming and, hoping to ease the tension, I started to cluck also. This did nothing. I propped the outside door open and went around the outside of the house banging on the windows to encourage him to make his get away, but to no avail. He was nice and warm in there.

It was about this time that my son called with, "What are you up to, mom?"

"Cant talk now, I am trying to coax a squirrel out of my friends house."

"Really? Are you in some kind of movie?"

With no luck we decided to bring in help. The next day, armed with a wiffle-ball bat and a hockey stick a friend of ours stopped by to get the key to the squirrel-infested house.

"GOOD LUCK!" I shouted as he drove off.

Later that day I got the call that the mission was accomplished. He said, "I chased that thing all over. At one point he jumped at me and I had to roll around on the floor. I sure wish I had taken a tennis racket."

Laughing hysterically I told him I wish I had been there. When I finally regained my composure I asked him if he had gotten it on video.

My city squirrels are brown fat and fluffy, sort of cute. My lake squirrels are skinny and black and have a very bad attitude. As I was trying to exit my cottage one day I was bombarded by a group of about 20 of these rambunctious creatures. I think they must have spent the night in a field of really bad mushrooms. They were crazy. They were swinging from trees, window sills and each other. A bouncer made it very clear that I would not be leaving the cottage until he said so. It was quite obvious I would not be interfering with their party. I could call the local law but what would I say? "I am being held hostage by a bunch of squirrels?" I am sure a call like that could get you on some sort of list, and not in a good way. Eventually they got bored and marched off to intimidate some other unsuspecting neighbor.

For such a small creature they must have a very large brain. No matter what plan I come up with to keep them out of the bird feeder they seem to come up with a better plan. How do they do it? Maybe there is a squirrel engineer up there in that nest. My last-ditch effort was to lace a slinky down the bird feeder pole. It was pretty funny watching those little creatures bounce up and down.

Some might say these little creatures are just rats with tails that go around causing all kinds of damage and in some cases they may be right, but on the other hand I have found them quite entertaining. Of course if I were to notice they had chewed a hole in my new siding I may have another opinion.

FAMILY TRADITIONS

The coconut doesn't roll far from the tree which will explain a lot. As the years go by I have come to the realization that my family may have been a bit twisted. Being raised in a town of around 300 and most of them relatives could explain a lot.

Mother's job was to keep us on the straight and narrow and our job was to let her, or so she thought. At times mother could be very entertaining in a somewhat scary way. She had dreams and nightmares that she would participate in, literally. One night she dreamed she was sitting on a platform watching the trains go by and when she woke up she had managed to get dad to sit with her. They were both sleeping. One night she woke up in the yard, under the apple tree with her pajamas in her hand. There goes the neighborhood.

Cursing was not allowed at any time in our home. That rule went out the window when during one of mom's bad nights she would fly down the hallway cursing like a drunken sailor for no apparent reason. That pretty much ended overnight guests for my brother and me.

Mom was happy, for the most part, but the weather scared her. If there was a cloud in the sky you could bet we would be spending the day indoors under mother hen's wing. If a storm actually did appear it was down to the basement with a metal pail over our heads in case of flying glass. Are you kidding? If that actually happened, you can bet we would be rendered deaf for the rest of our lives. When the wind blew it was off to the neighbors tornado shelter. Yes, they had an actual shelter built under the ground for just such an occasion. Sometimes half of the town would be in that shelter, all except mother. One thing that scared her more than storms was the fear of being trapped underground. I guess her role was to watch the storm and let us all know when we would be motherless.

Dad worked six days a week in retail and on the seventh day he rebuilt appliances in the garage to sell. He did the outside jobs and managed in his spare time to build us a house. I liked to hang out with dad and learned a lot about electricity, plumbing, and so on. This came in handy when I married someone who knew nothing about such things. To this day I still have a skill saw, chop saw, and all the power tools. The small town we lived in was pretty much lower class or middle class so we were all pretty much in the same boat. With very little contact with the outside world we were quite aware when a stranger should roll into town. We had our door-to-door salesmen peddling their wares including Godly fellows who came to save our souls and sell us huge ornate bibles that no one could afford.

I had one brother who was almost seven years younger than me. I'm pretty sure I was excited when I heard we were going to have a new baby in the house although I have been told when I got the news that a new baby brother was on his way home from the hospital I ran into the back yard and pulled grass. Hmm, maybe I really liked being an only child. I adjusted and that summer I pushed him around town in my doll buggy dressed like a girl. Maybe all that grass pulling was because I really wanted a sister.

Turned out my brother was a blessing. He was the class clown and kept our family laughing. He was only eleven when I got married and left home but we still tell Rick stories when we get together. He also kept mother busy so I had lots of time to enjoy all my small town had to offer.

We were lucky as my mother thought kids should be kids, giving us time to play and exercise our imaginations. She felt we had the rest of our lives to be grownups and we would never be children again. Childhood was something we could never relive. I treasure those childhood memories and will always be grateful for them.

Thanks Mom.

HOME REPAIRS

I have to admire anyone who is a do-it-yourself-er. Dad did it all: plumbing, electrical, remodeling, rebuilt TVs and resold them from the garage. I like to think this apple didn't fall far from the tree, but I would be wrong. While Dad was a "Jack of all trades and master of all" I, on the other hand, am "Jack of all trades and master of none." I give it my best.

How hard can it be to paint a room? Open a can, stick in a brush and spread it on the wall. There is this thing called preparation; I skip right over that part. It's kind of like not reading the instructions, which is only done as a last resort and by then they are at the bottom of the trash covered with leftovers. Yuck!

I did discover that using the electric sander too close to the smoke detector causes it to scream its lungs out until you get a ladder, locate a crowbar and physically rip the thing from the wall. Guess the batteries aren't dead after all.

I try to be careful so there will be no need for a drop cloth. You could slip and twist an ankle, or even worse. Besides, if you leave a few spatters along the way you will always be reminded of what the room used to look like when you repaint. Of course, walking around in your bare feet after stepping on the paint-can lid has the same effect.

I like to get right at the job, so I see no need to clear a room. I move the furniture as I go. There is that off-chance that you may paint yourself into a corner for what seems like an eternity but have no fear, these new fast-drying paints should set you free in an hour or so. Stair-steps are always a challenge. I tried that idea of painting every other one all the way to the top and using the unpainted ones to find my way back to the bottom. Make no mistake, if by accident you should step on a painted one you may find yourself at the bottom faster than you expected and probably not in an upright position.

Electrical work can be tricky. One false move and you may be laying out flat in a sea of flowers. I always solicited my husband in these little projects. If I'm going on any extended trips I want him to go too. We gave these jobs over to a professional the day we turned the light off in the bathroom and it came on in the kitchen. To this day, the on-switches mean OFF and the off-switches mean ON. Now for someone like me who doesn't know if I'm coming or going, it all makes perfect sense.

Plumbing is not my favorite job. There is nothing more challenging than trying to fit two water pipes together. First you have to turn yourself into a pretzel, hold a flashlight in your teeth, drag a bag of wrenches, none of which will fit anything, and crawl into a space barely large enough for a chipmunk. The pipe will be too short or too long and after hours of trying to figure it out you head to the local hardware and discover the flexible pipe. I could not believe it! I was so excited, I nearly kissed this guy full on the mouth. A flexible pipe that will bend anyway you want it to. Best invention ever since the "Bent-handled Snow Shovel."

We felt the need to change something about every house we have ever owned. By the time we finished remodeling our first house we were facing a new street and had a new address. There were walls we put in new that we ended up taking out. It was a 20 year running project. There was a rumor of a previous owner who had been a wealthy man. It seems he died penniless, and I was sure the money was hidden in the walls of that house.

One little noise here or there and out came the sledge hammer followed by patching plaster. The solid concrete steps were the last to go. We all stood by waiting for the big reveal as the air hammer chipped away at the concrete. Disappointment was obvious as the last stone was turned and all we found was dust, I had the feeling that old fellow was somewhere having the last laugh. But I had high hopes. I started digging up the back yard when the park down the street was being excavated for Indian artifacts. Those little mounds of dirt in the back yard had to mean something, right? I guess sometimes dirt is just dirt.

The last house we bought needed a lot of changes. Now, my husband was a dreamer. I would submit my plan and his dream was that I would forget all about it. Really, after so many years together he should know better. I measured the kitchen, ordered the cupboards, and found a guy with a truck to deliver them. All that dreaming went to the roadside when I got the hammer out and started destroying the old kitchen. Mission accomplished

I have all of the tools. So far I haven't sustained any serious bodily injuries. I did ask for hedge trimmers for mother's day one year and my daughter said there was no way. My husband's favorite fix-all was duct tape and over the years I have learned to appreciate its versatility.

My dad was a block and I am just a chip but I think he would give me a high mark for giving this whole "I can do it" thing a whirl.

HUMOR APPROPRIATE AND INAPPROPRIATE

L et me begin by saying my wonder years were spent singing to frogs, hanging upside down in trees and soaring high in my rope swing talking to God, whom up until the age of five I thought flew around heaven in an airplane. A vivid imagination is the forerunner to a good sense of humor, giving you the ability to see certain situations in a more askew way. I think my ancestors had an extra chromosome in the giggle department and it was a gene that has been passed on for generations. Laughter is contagious; you cannot look at a guy bent over in gut wrenching laughter and keep a straight face. It is just not possible. Neither can laughter be suppressed. It pops up in some of the most inappropriate times such as church, weddings, hospitals and even funerals which is totally inappropriate.

While visiting my daughter during the Christmas Holiday it was agreed that we would attend Christmas Eve service. It was a very small church that sat in the middle of town. It could seat 100 people at best and I am pretty sure it seldom hit capacity. The front door led directly into the sanctuary and once the congregation was seated and the doors closed, the only exit was next to the pulpit making it impossible to leave without every questioning eye upon you. If you did not attend church service regularly, Christmas and Easter were your "get home free cards." This was the perfect time for families to redeem themselves so we knew it would be a full house. We planned on getting there early and blend in with the crowd but best laid plans can run amok. When we arrived, the church was pretty well packed and it appeared the only vacant seat was in the front row. We made do and with a little adjusting we all found our spot. Elbow to elbow we sat with no wiggle room.

The last person to enter the sanctuary

was a rather robust lady frantically looking for a suitable place to park. She eventually ended up standing at the end of our pew. What to do, what to do? The words, "no room at the inn" echoed in the hollows of my mind. We all looked to each other for a solution but it was obvious we would all have to spare an inch or two and make room for this lady in distress. We were now packed in like a can of sardines, but room was made. We do a lot of standing and sitting in our church and it seemed each time we tried to return to our seat there was pew shrinkage. Man, that last lady was fast, she could reclaim her spot in a New York minute. Eventually there just wasn't room for all of us and I was left last man standing. It seemed the whole service was on hold waiting for me to find my place. I scanned the room for an alternative. The front entrance was closed and if anyone even thought of making a getaway they would have to deal with the church police in their three piece suits and candy cane ties. With all eyes on me and blushing with embarrassment I looked to my family for a solution. What was I thinking? There they were all looking at me with that ear to ear grin and I knew I was on my own. The giggle bug bit me and I did the only thing I could do. I bolted past the pulpit, headed straight for the ladies room where I stuffed my mouth with paper towel and peed down my leg. Not my best moment.

Losing it in church is not a new thing with me. I was kicked out of choir as a teen because I couldn't keep it together. Oh well, I couldn't carry a tune anyway... which over the years has brought great laughter to my closest friends.

There are two great things about being invited to a distant friends wedding.

ONE: you will see a few people you know, and TWO: most of the people don't know you so if you fall flat on your face or drink directly from the toilet it's no big deal. No reference, no name, no problem. You are off the hook.

I attended such a wedding with another anonymous couple a few years ago. The bride and groom had dedicated one year of their lives to making plans for this blissful day. The family would be clad in their Sunday best and close friends and relatives would have received their invitations well in advance, giving them plenty of time to RSVP and shop for the perfect gift. Sooner than they thought the big day would be upon them. The church would be filled with the aroma of fresh cut bouquets. The end of each isle would be decorated with ribbon and candles. The bride had chosen the perfect gown and the groom stood ready with ring in hand pledging to put his bachelor days behind him. The ushers, in their rented tux, would lead the guests to their seats. Bride's side? Groom's side? The minister would stand at the pulpit ready to help them tie the knot. The music will play, 'Here comes the bride,' as necks will crank to see the bride being escorted down the aisle in her gorgeous gown and flowing veil. This day has been lived and relived several times. What could go wrong?

As we exited the car in the church parking lot, the heat hit us like a brick. It was 100 degrees. Oh boy, hot and humid. With any luck the church would be air-conditioned. That would be a no. We bypassed the ushers and we were lucky to discover seats in the very back row, that way if any one of us fainted from heat exhaustion we could be carried out with hardly anyone knowing. The service began and things were rolling along as planned. The bride and groom held hands as they waited anxiously for the Wedding Singer to do his stuff. We sat fanning ourselves with our programs in anticipation. Now, it takes a lot of courage to sing at a wedding. I can barely pull it off in the shower. The singer had a beautiful voice but he and the music had nothing in common. The singer and the music could have been at two different weddings. We were all thinking eventually they might meet somewhere in the middle but it just went on and on with no end in sight. A mind reader could have read our thoughts. Good Lord, is there no end to this torture? Then my friend whispered, "I didn't know it was karaoke night." That's all it took. The heat and tenseness of the moment over took us and we just couldn't hold it in any longer. Total uncontrollable hysteria over took us.

Exit left. We jumped ship like a pack of drowning rats. Heard the marriage was a bust. Maybe it was the music.

Small churches, hot summer days and weddings seem to be a breeding ground for me to tap into that giggle gene. I, along with my mother and husband, were invited to a family wedding. This is no place to screw up. Family remembers everything and they never let you forget. The bride was marrying her first husband's brother. We all liked the first husband but agreed the brother was a better choice and wished them many years of happiness. The kids were all grown up and I am sure at first it was a stretch to have your uncle become your step-dad but good news was they kept the same grandparents. The wedding was to be held in a quaint country church. It was another extremely hot summer day with only family and close friends attending and it was allergy season. Heat, humidity and allergies; nothing good can come from this. Halfway through the ceremony my eyes started itching and my nose started running. I could feel a sonic boom sneeze coming. I could picture every stained glass window in this little church being blown into the next county. That's when I tried to suppress the beast with a tight pinch to the upper nostril. This caused any air that might have escaped to make a loud sound that one could only associate with the other end of ones body. That sound echoed off every wall. Heads turned, including mine. My mother looked at me and said, "some things never change." Not helping.

By now my husband had moved into another pew. I thought my insides would burst as mother and I choked back the laughter and I could only hope my tears would be perceived as sentimental emotion. Little beads of sweat started to form on my forehead and my curly hair looked more like a wet bale of hay. The ceremony seemed to go on for eternity. When it was over I just hoped the incident would not be mentioned at the reception. I was wrong. My cousin was the first to say, "Did anyone hear that humongous fart?" And then they had the gall to laugh about it.

As my husband was about to tell all I gave

him the death wish look and interceded with, "unbelievable."

Laughter is a good thing. I don't know too many people without a sense of humor nor would I want to. Laughter really is the best medicine. It has gotten me over some rough spots and provided our family with memories that go on forever.

Getting the giggles at a funeral is not only inappropriate, it is ludicrous. Tears and laughter are very strong emotions and sometimes the laughter helps ease the moment. Well, that's my take anyway.

In a nearby town where my Aunt Wanda lived was the Miller Funeral Home which had been in the funeral business ever since I could remember. They were generational. If you were a member of my family and you still lived in the vicinity it was a given that you would be meeting your maker via the Millers. Dot and Pete Miller would be the last people on earth who would see you naked.

My Aunt Wanda never missed reading the daily obits and I know she kept a tally because she called to give me the updates:

Pete and Dot were getting up there in years, and it was said that Pete's memory was not what it should be, and everyone was wondering just who was embalming the bodies? Aunt Wanda's fear was that Dot and Pete would bite the dust before she did and where on earth was she supposed to go? This did not happen. As we all gathered around Wanda's bed to bid our farewells we assured her that we would call Dot and Pete as soon as she breathed her last breath. The time came and our caregiver made the call.

It was 2AM and the conversation went something like this: "Hello Dot, I am calling to tell you that Wanda Green just passed away at her home."

Dot replied, "Who? Wanda Green? Pete, wake up! Wanda Green just died."

Then she said to the caregiver, "Are there any men there that can help us? Are there any steps we have to go up?"

We assured her that we could easily lift our 98 pound aunt and there were only two steps. After the caregiver hung up I said I would pass out cold if I saw Dot come up our sidewalk. Not long after the call a van pulled up (who knows where they left the hearse) and here came Dot walking up the sidewalk.

I turned to the girls and said, "get the smelling salts." It was 2AM and Dot looked like a 100 year old Barbie doll. She was wearing nylons and heels, a starched blouse and a mid calf skirt. Her hair was a mile high and a class-6 tornado couldn't have moved it.

We all looked at each other and the caregiver headed to the bathroom. I pictured her sitting on the side of the tub, holding her sides trying to stifle the laughter. We tried to keep it together as the Millers entered the house and gave their condolences. Pete zipped Wanda into a black bag in front of us all. Then the caregiver interceded by unzipping the bag so we could say our last goodbyes.

Now it was time to get Wanda into the van. My niece took one end of the gurney while my daughter pushed a relieved Pete out of the way and took the other end, and out the door they went. As they loaded Aunt Wanda into the van my daughter leaned over and said, "you wanted Millers and you got Millers."

We made it through the funeral without incident. After a nice luncheon and condolences from family and friends we returned to the funeral home to distribute the flowers and plants. A couple of weeks had passed when my daughter-in-law called to let me know she found a pair of glasses in her plant. Did I have any idea who they might belong to? Sure enough they were Dots. We all miss Aunt Wanda but we all still get a chuckle out of the story.

My husband Dale had a wonderful sense of humor. He had to or we wouldn't have stayed married 47 years. He died at the age of 65 which was way too soon. I asked the hospital to contact our local funeral director and I would call them the next day to make arrangements. We were all devastated but there are always those unbelievable instances that creep in and keep you going. Most of them make you smile even in the worst of times.

Our local funeral home was owned by friends and I knew they would be shocked when they heard of Dales passing. I called the next day to make an appointment to meet with them and they were shocked all right. They had not heard the news, and worse yet: they did not have him. What? How could this be?

I was sure I had given instructions to the hospital the night before. It had not been 12 hours and I had lost my husbands body.

I remember the hospital saying something about taking him to Bells which was a restaurant nearby but I knew that couldn't be, could it? Was he sitting somewhere in a parking lot waiting to be picked up? My kids were a tad concerned but not a bit surprised that I could lose dad.

After a few hours of panic it was true the hospital did say Bells. Because he died in a different county the coroner from that county had to be called to pronounce him deceased, so he was taken to Bells Funeral Home next door to the hospital to be transferred later that day. Whew, what a relief! A few tense hours but a story that lives on.

Through all of our grief and tears there

were those "pop up moments," that softened the blow. Our back yard joined the yard of a retirement home and during that time they were having a carnival with a hillbilly band playing all day and into the night. We all sat on the porch and thought about how much dad would have loved it. What a send off.

A couple long days at a funeral home can be exhausting but when you think you can't do it anymore a "get in your face" gal comes in and goes on about how she just could not believe Dale was gone. My daughter Jeana and I were at the casket and out of the corner of your eyes we saw this gal get closer and closer to my daughter Robbin, backing her further and further into the flower arrangements. We both thought for sure the arrangements would go down, taking Robbin with them. The thought certainly lightened the moment. We couldn't hold back.

Later Robbin said she believes that was the 5 minutes God gave dad to look up and see his family and what did he see? He saw the two of you hanging over the casket laughing. Of course that just made us laugh harder. Later that night my mother wanted to know who that drunk gal was who tried to bury Robbin in the flower arrangements. Mother assumed everyone out of the ordinary had to be tipping the bottle.

Finally the day of the funeral was here and with the support of family and friends we headed to the church. We were pretty shook up as we stood to sing the first song. My daughter Robbin has a beautiful voice but Jeana and I... well, not so much.

As Robbin gave a glare at Jeana who was not singing, Jeana whispered, "Dad liked it better if I didn't sing."

Tensions were high and that's all it took. Sweat was running down my neck as I kept saying to myself, "For Gods sake, you have lost it at your husbands funeral. My brother said he saw our shoulders moving and he knew we were crying and then he wasn't too sure."

After the funeral the funeral director put his arm around me and told me how sorry he was and said it seemed like only yesterday we were all in high school and I was a cheerleader.

I told him I was never a cheerleader and he said, "yes you were."

"Okay," I replied. "I guess I was." After what I had been through I guess I deserved to be a cheerleader.

Dale would have expected no less from us. It's been a long time since he left us and we love to sit around and tell "Dale stories." We sure do miss him and his sense of humor. He had the ability to see the brighter side of life in about everything. It's there even when times are rough.

WATER
WONDER LAND

Ever since I can remember I have been obsessed with water, which is surprising since I never learned to swim until I was an adult. I grew up in a town in the middle of Michigan called Riverdale. It was a small community with a population of 300 or less. This little berg was rightly named as it was perched on the banks of the Pine River. I spent many long hot summer days with my best friend, laying in the long grasses along the bank watching the flowing waters make their way to the mighty ocean, a place we had only read about. If we were lucky, my mother would load up the neighborhood kids and take us to a nearby lake for the day. Even though it was a small inland lake I would imagine the waters could carry me away to foreign lands. The thrill of large masses of water has never left. Little did I know where it would take me!

If you are going to be on the water I believe you should literally be on the water.

In our early camping years I floated around on a $1 rubber raft. That was wonderful but as time passed I started longing for something with a wee bit more speed. I had the urge to get farther from the beach so I started scoping out boats.

There she was, sitting beside the road just waiting for me to come along. She was a red and white Imperial with a huge outboard motor. Knowing absolutely nothing about watercraft, I solicited the advice of a friend who had more knowledge than I did (which was nada). Let the fun begin.

Having never owned a boat before made me realize I had best take a class and bone up on watercraft regulations. I gathered up all my teenage friends that I assumed would want to take their turn at the wheel and we enrolled in a boater safety class. That's right, just me and a bunch of thirteen year olds. I already decided if I flunked the final exam I would have to move to another country. I passed.

I had a lot of fun with that boat but it did have an attitude. I decided since I had a boaters permit I deserved an upgrade. My boss suggested I attend a boat show and see just what was out there. I didn't buy a boat there but I pretty much knew, down the line there would be a boat in my future. My boss bought a pair of skis and he didn't even own a watercraft.

Sure enough, within a month we were sitting at a marina checking out a beautiful brand-new Four Winds Boat.

"Well," my boss asked, "what do you think?"

What could I say? It was beautiful, but where was I going to get the money?

"Not a problem," my boss assured me. He explained that I could get a loan and although he didn't pay me enough to get a loan that size, he was my boss and could tell the loan officer any number they needed. Besides, it was about time I established my own credit rating. How could you argue with genius like that? I was pretty sure he went right home and put an extra coat of wax on his skies.

Dale and I had been married for several years and absolutely nothing I did surprised him by this point. When I told him that Bob and I went to look at boats and I bought one, he replied "That's nice."

I got the call that my boat was ready to be picked up. I asked Dale to meet me at the marina. He stood there, looking up at my boat. It looked like the Titanic sitting on the boat trailer.

He did stammer a bit as he greeted me: "What have you done now?"

I assured him it would look a lot smaller in the water and how nice it was that the dealer had arranged for us to take a trial run on a nearby river. He declined.

I felt a lot less guilty after he found a little red pontoon that he could park at the lake (and watch me fly by in my new boat). God, I loved that man.

As the years passed the kids grew up. We bought our lakefront property. Another boat show found me selling my boat and purchasing a beautiful 24 foot pontoon. I felt just like Cleopatra every noon as Dale took us on our daily tour of the lake. Life was good. Since Dale has passed away and I have the place to myself, I sold the big boat and am back to a Micky Mouse raft I bought for $1 at the dollar store. I did mention to a dear neighbor that it would be nice to have a boat.

He said in no uncertain terms "You're not getting a boat."

Kayaks seem to be rather popular these days. That might be just what I need. I am 4 feet 10 inches tall, so the seawall makes the shore water about thigh-high. How on earth could I ever get in a kayak without flipping it? A friend told me she just sits on her dock and slides in. You have to be kidding. I am short. I can not reach a kayak from my dock. If I could, I am sure the kayak would float off and I would hit my head on the dock and be rendered unconscious. I'd drown! There has to be a better way.

I decided to borrow my neighbors kayak for a week to see how I liked it. I have a nice set of stairs leading into the water, so I thought I could just pull the kayak up to them and slide right in. It worked perfectly until I realized the back of the seat was down and I was sitting on top of it. No problem; I'll just inch my way into the hull and pull the seat into place. This was a very bad idea.

Boom! I am upside down in the lake and the kayak is full of water. A half hour later after I had dragged the kayak out, drained it and got it back in the water I started over with the back of the seat upright. To my amazement, I slid right in again. I think I have this down pat.

That's when I noticed the life jacket was still on shore. No problem, I'll just nail it with the oar. Actually, to my surprise it worked. I am off! Once I got to my friends house across the lake I would have it made. She had a pull-up beach and I could just ram myself unto dry land.

She ran down to greet me. With wide eyed panic I called out to her "KEEP AWAY FROM THE BOAT. I have this!"

I paddled for all I was worth and assumed I was far enough towards shore, so I rose to gracefully exit the boat. Never assume. The boat flipped and I came up covered with mud wearing a lily pad hat.

After my friend regained her composure she hosed me off and asked if she could load up the kayak and give me a ride home.

"Oh no," I said. "The trip back will be a piece of cake." Yeah, it was upstream but it was a calm day. Just as I started home, up came the wind and a nice summer storm. Yikes!

I hung tight to the shore and prayed the whole way. I can swim but I doubt I could swim while dragging the kayak. How would I ever tell my neighbors the kayak was at the bottom of the lake? When will I learn to actually put the life jacket on?

I made it home eventually. When my neighbor came up on the weekend and asked how it went I told her it was great. It was so great I was thinking of getting my own kayak. I see people out there every day and on cooler days they actually have their clothes and jackets on. How on earth do they do that without getting wet?

There must be a guy who spends his time

going from cottage to cottage with a big lift truck and lifts them in. I am sure he only works after dark as I have never really seen him.

How about a canoe? Maybe that will be my next big adventure.

DRIVING

I grew up in a rural community where if you were old enough to walk you were given permission to drive a tractor. My best friend's dad sold tractors so every time we got the chance we would lift one off the lot and ride around town. She drove and I stood on the back and we thought we were pretty cool until her father would discover one of his tractors missing and send someone to retrieve it which gave us cause to go back to riding our bikes and dream of the day when we could drive.

In this small town of approximately 300 most of us were relatives. No law enforcement, no curbs, no traffic. Therefore one could drive when one was tall enough to see over the steering wheel. Barely being able to do this I began double clutching an old clunker around town at age 14. If, for some uncanny reason, the Sheriff should show up I just left the car parked and walked the one block home. He never stayed long and I could always go back later.

Just before I was legally old enough to drive my father purchased a 1956 Mercury and being the wheeler-and-dealer he was they tossed in an old beater for $50. It was a Plymouth. We dubbed them the BIG M and the LITTLE P. I thought it was the most beautiful car I had ever seen. In one year I would manage to have several flat tires, lose all the chrome trim and encourage my best friend to hang out the window in pouring rain to manually operate the broken windshield wipers. The day of my 16th birthday my father drove me to the county seat where I got my legal drivers license, at which time he handed me the keys to the LITTLE P, turned me loose with a car load of giggling teen age girls and set me adrift in a town much larger than mine where I proceeded to drive over every curb and sidewalk. Oh the glory days of youth. Over the years we have traded automobiles several times and each one leaves us with a memorable tale.

Dale and I didn't have a car when we got married. We borrowed his mother's car the night we got married but had to have it home the next day so she could go to work. Needless to say we didn't travel far for a one night honeymoon. Our first car was our pride and joy. Just how much rust do you think you can get for $200 in the 50s? The answer would be, enough to see you through your first year of marriage. Next we had a Ford Falcon. The governor at that time had one too, and I felt like royalty. Then I drove it through the driveway gate with the doors wide open. Why I would back out of the drive with the doors open is still a mystery to me but that day I discovered what the rear view mirror was for. The doors on that car — along with the gate — never fit just right after that little incident.

Our first brand new, hot off the line, Olds Cutlass was beautiful. My husband worked for General Motors and hand picked every part. Oh, he went on and on about this new car and could not wait for me to take it for a spin. He rode shotgun and criticized my every turn of the wheel. After a few blocks I spun back into the drive, flung the door open forgetting the basketball pole. Whoops! A couple pails of ice water will bring anyone around. I really did feel bad but he never offered to ride with me again.

Let's not forget the car stuck on the side of the house. You know: house too close to the ice covered driveway, car slides into house, you get the picture. My daughter was distraught as she was behind the wheel when this all went down. Oh posh, not to worry, I'll fix this. Back and forth, and a little dent turns into a long gash. Now daughter is sobbing, and that's when I came up with a plan. Put the blame on dad. Sure he was 60 miles away at work, but this was one of those "listen and learn" lessons every girl should know. As he walked in the door, and before he could say a word I hit him with. "I hope you are happy, if you had just taken the time to shovel the drive, none of this would have happened."

Over the years I have managed to strand one auto on top of a mound of snow with all 4 wheels up in the air, been hauled out of a farmers field taking a short cut to a friend's house, ran into telephone poles, parked autos in garage doors. I left the base off an old time bumper jack and pumped the thing 12 inches into the ground trying to change a tire. I have hit 3 deer, but will go in the ditch trying to avoid smaller critters.

One day I discovered a small bubble just to the front of my rear tire. I assumed it was some pitch from the pine tree. Hum, guess I will just pull that off. As hard as I tried to get it off, it was not giving an inch. Where are my needle nose pliers? Well it came off alright along with a huge piece of plastic coating. Geez, I guess you learn something new every day. Who knew that fender was encased in a coat of plastic. Guess I had better head out to the local Auto Repair Shop. Being in a hurry I cut across a mini mall parking lot and out of the corner of my eye I saw the perfect parking spot. What I didn't see was that handicap sign on a pole incased in a ton of concrete. I managed to move it a whole parking space. Now instead of being able to park a handicap car, you could actually park a handicap bus. Feeling like I should report this unfortunate incident to someone I headed to city hall. The clerk could see I was a tad distraught so she asked what she could do for me. With a gulp I blurted out, "I'm here to find out who owns the handicap signs in the parking lot just north of town?"

She looked a bit puzzled but went on to ask me why I wanted to know. I continued with, "Well, I moved one."

Her expression was priceless. She had no idea where these signs came from, but said she would pass the word on. Well, I figured I had done my duty telling someone so I headed to the Auto Repair Shop again.

Now over the years we had a magic substance that fixed everything. That substance was BOND-O. We had owned cars that were more BOND-O than steel. I don't know how General Motors missed this but I think they could actually build a complete car with this stuff. I'm sure this repair shop would have barrels of it and I was thinking this would be a cheap fix. I guess it had been a few years since I had visited an auto repair shop and to my surprise I discovered our new autos are pretty much plastic toys and I doubt if the attendant had ever heard of Bond-o. Not a good start to my day. Why repair anything when you can just replace it? Guess General Motors didn't need my suggestion about Bond-o after all. If you think these plastic parts are going to be inexpensive you can think again. Way too much money so I guess the old girl will have to live with a few wrinkles.

I was shocked the day I backed out of the garage and ripped the outside mirror off the driver's side of the car. I can only contribute this to garage door shrinkage. Well that and the fact that I am a terrible backer upper. I had the mirror replaced. I figured if I had a hard time going backwards with the mirror on, it would be impossible with it off.

One day while I was getting my oil changed the auto dealer was observing the cars dents and chips, and broken parts. I looked him in the eye and told him I assumed after seeing how careless I was with my vehicle I was sure he would never place another in my care. He assured me he had no problem selling me another and he really didn't care what happen after money had been exchanged and papers were signed. That seemed a tad heartless.

Amazingly up to this date I have not had an accident. That's not to say I may not have caused a few. Once I saw a guy in the ditch shaking his fist at me so I just waved back.

No, most of my problems start when I step out of the car. Example: Assuming my car was in park, I left it running while I stepped out long enough to move a bucket in the garage. Never assume. I thought I was having some kind of out of body experience as, out of the corner of my eye I saw my car slowly creeping down the drive. I was able to grab the door handle, which caused the door to swing open and now I am face down bouncing over tiny mountains of snow. Wouldn't you think at some point I may have thought about letting go of the handle? Not a chance. Then the strangest thing happened, the car is still moving but I was not but I still had the handle in my hand. What? Was this possible? I am a grandmother and I have just ripped the door handle off my car. The boys at the garage got a big laugh over this antic and when I left they wanted to know what I intended to do next. I told them I thought I would leap off a tall building as it seemed I had super powers.

This was not the first time my car had gotten away from me. The time before my car not only drove itself down the drive but was involved in an accident. The lady in the other car said she blew her horn but the beast just kept coming. An officer was called and he thought I should get a ticket, but he wasn't sure what crime I had committed so he went back to his office to read up on the situation and sent me a citation in the mail for not having my car under control. I really do not know how this could be as I was on the porch at the time.

I'm not even going to explain the dent in my mother's garage door. It seems my vehicle has a mind of its own when I am not around. Maybe I should ground it and take its keys away.

When my son turned 16 he was handed the keys to our second car. It was a Mercury Grand Marquee handed down from grandpa, as big as a Sherman Tank. Turned out this was just what he needed as he ran into just about everything in town.

We were putting up our Christmas décor when our son Randy walked in with a guy we assumed was a friend. It seems they were involved in a fender bender down the block and neither one of them knew what to do so they just walked home to tell us. Oh, it was going to be a long year.

He took out a mailbox, backed into a parked car and who knows what else. The funny thing is, that big old tank hardly had a scratch on it.

We were totally prepared when our daughter Robbin turned 16 and started to drive. To our great surprise she never even got a parking ticket. She kept the car clean and always returned it with more gas than before. Who is this kid?

Eight years later our daughter Jeana took the wheel and we began having Randy flashbacks. She called her dad to tell him she had a flat tire but when he got there they were loading the car on a flat bed truck with all four tires pointing in different directions.

Just love the fact that she didn't over react. She left that to dad.

When this mode of travel was invented the auto makers promised us an automobile in every garage but today it seems everyone in the family has their own. Then there is the one that resembles a bus that sits in the driveway just in case the family should all have to travel together. Love them or hate them it seems we all need them. Not like the days of yore when a guy took his horse and buggy to the local tavern and when he had tipped one too many, some kind comrade would load him up, give the horse a whack on the butt and the horse would take the poor sot home, safe and sound. Now there's a concept I could live with. Of course every now and then the horse would get confused and end up sticking his head through some poor soul's screen door.

JUST ONE OF THOSE DAYS

They say as you get older you have a tendency to forget things. I must have been born old. There is no stopping off in my brain, no processing center, and no u-turns. I think half of what we hear is nonsense so keep what you like and toss the rest. The last time I was at the doctors I was read a two minute story, cute little story but when they asked me the name of the girl in the story I didn't have a clue, and who cares. To this day I remember the story. Another cute little test to see if you brought your brain with you or left it home, is to draw a clock that reads 11:10. I know their goal is to have you draw the hands on the clock but I always have the urge to write the digital time. But then again I also like living unassisted.

After you pass these two little tests — or not — you get to see the doctor. When he asked me how I had been the past year I replied, "Let me see... After living in the same town for 60 years I sold my house and took four months to move all my stuff to my lake cottage which was not livable in the winter, so I hired a crew to build a new house with plans I drew myself. I selected every cabinet, counter top, floor board, window, light fixture, and so forth. During this time I spent 3 months living with my boyfriend, then I drove an hour to come here and draw you a clock."

The look on Docs face was priceless especially since I just failed the clock thing.

Actually there were times during this whole process that I wondered why my children hadn't tried to stop me so I asked them. They said, "Mom, you always talk through the top of your head so we didn't think you would actually do it." I do wonder how I pulled it all off. You are never too old and it's never too late, or maybe I just got lucky.

My friends say I don't listen and when I

do I just screw it all up. I think they may be on to something. While out to dinner one evening one of my friends was telling about visiting a nursing home and how she had seen her friend, Agnes, nude, standing in the hallway. My reply, "Don't think I know her... No, I never knew any Nudes." All eyes turned on me as I continued, "I really cannot remember the Nude family. Did they go to our church?"

Once I went out for the evening and came home with only one shoe, and I have been looking for my ecru jacket for a good 15 years now. I can lay a hammer down in the kitchen and not be able to find it for a couple days. A hammer is not a small item.

I have gone to Tupperware parties a week early and baby showers a week late.

On Monday I replaced the battery in my kitchen clock and reset it. Tuesday I realized the microwave clock was off. Wednesday it was the bedroom clock. On Friday I reset the outside clock. Do you see a pattern here? Wouldn't you have thought that at some point I may have asked myself why all of these clocks needed resetting, or perhaps the first clock might have been wrong? It was Saturday when I checked my phone and I realized I'd been a half hour early all week. Yes, my whole week had been a LIE in time land.

I was sure I had gone to the other side when I glanced at my bedroom clock and it read 80:01. A closer look and I discovered the clock was upside down and it was really 10:08. That's what happens when you dust.

Sometimes I get so distracted I will be dusting the piano and then I am playing the piano which puts me in a mood to play guitar and the next thing you know I have walked over the feather duster for three days. Oh, I knew it was there. I guess it was just not on my list of priorities.

Switching from a landline to a cellular phone was quite an adventure. I had my home phone number transferred to my new, ever so convenient, cellular just in case someone should call me, thinking I was home, and I could actually tell them I was on a tropical island. Believe me, this will never happen. I did get a call from a friend to go to lunch once and I had the pleasure of telling her I was in Florida and then I asked her how the weather was in Michigan. Love this new phone.

As we all know these phones require a different password for every function. I was told this password was top secret stuff. I felt like I left the place with a bottle of kryptonite and if I lost it some super hero was going to die. Now for someone who can't remember what she had for lunch this is a huge responsibility. My first thought was to have all these passwords tattooed backwards on my back side so I could read them in the mirror.

One day I took this mysterious little gadget to the phone center with a list of questions. A very pleasant young lady took my phone and then asked the impossible, "What's your password?" After reciting a bunch of meaningless words I just threw in the towel and got a new phone, went home and wrote that password on everything in the house.

Ever misplace your cellphone? Now there's a panic attack of gigantic proportion. My whole life is in mine. How many times do you think it is appropriate to go to your neighbors in your PJs and ask them to call you when you got home so you can locate that which is lost? A friend of mine lost his cellphone and had to call his mother — in another state — from his office to get my number so he could call me for help. While he retraced his steps from the night before, I called him from the car, the driveway and finally from his house where I found the phone under some papers. Disaster averted. I think all cellphones should come equipped with the clapper, of course I probably wouldn't remember where I put it. In case my phone should get run over by a semi I have recorded all of my phone numbers on a yellow legal pad with a number 2 pencil and put it in a safe place. Hmm, I wonder where that safe place might be?

I think text messaging is a hoot. I sent a message to my son-in-law one day while he was at work and it went like this:

MESSAGE: David, get out the barf bag as I am about to watch that chick flick you hate.

ANSWER: Wrong number

MY REPLY: Oh yeah, if this is the wrong number how can you return my text?

ANSWER: Wrong number

MY REPLY: Ok, if this is the wrong number, what is your right number?

ANSWER: WRONG NUMBER!

It took awhile but I finally figured it out. This was not my son-in-law.

A friend of mine had some medical tests run and I text him to see if he had gotten any results. In my haste I sent the message to my other son-in-law who just happened to have the same name. When he received the message he pushed the panic button and immediately called my daughter to see what test results he was waiting for. She told him that he and I were the two most ditzy people she knew and that I was probably texting my friend with the same name. Note to self: add last name to all contacts.

Years ago there was only one day you could renew your vehicle license. It was a mad house. Each year my husband would send me down to stand in line and hopefully get a new (hammered out by prisoners) license plate for our car. When they asked me the make and model of the vehicle I usually said something like, "Car and Blue." Nothing ever went smoothly and he usually ended up taking a day off work to get them himself.

Then came the day I actually got it right. I was so proud of myself the year I walked out with my new plates. That afternoon the local police called to ask if I had gotten my plates earlier. Wow this must be a survey, "Yes I did," I said proudly. This call was definitely not a survey. It seems I had placed the plates on top of the car while fumbling for my keys and somewhere between here and there they had fallen off and now were at the police station. Close, so close.

I sit a lot of stuff on top of the car while I dig through my purse looking for those keys. I carelessly sat a pot roast on top of the car at my mothers once and amazingly made it all the way home without it sliding off. Thank God I never sat one of the kids up there. Through the years the cars got bigger and I got shorter and that problem seemed to take care of itself.

Do we really need a license for everything? Do you realize you could be buying a license almost every day? You need a license for your car and one that allows you to drive it. You need one for your boat, your boat trailer, and another to fish from it. What about your pets, or business? The list goes on and on and we have to keep track of them all because they all have to be renewed. Whew! The only license I can think of that is not renewable is your marriage license, and maybe we should rethink that one. I bet with that expiration date looming over head, attitudes could be adjusted real fast. Those who see no need to renew would save a lot of money in lawyer fees and the renewal fees could generate revenue for the state. Now, there's a thought.

Finding a good, up close, parking spot at the store is a gift. Of course this is only beneficial if you exit the door you entered. Nothing is more disturbing than coming out the wrong door and yelling, "Someone has stolen my car, and I had the best space ever."

One day I found the perfect parking spot. When I entered the store I had the weird feeling that every familiar display was in the wrong place. That's when I discovered I was at the wrong store. Rats! My odds of finding a spot like that at the other store would probably be nil to none.

Going to the laundromat can be a fun experience until you close your front loading washer door and as the water is rushing in you discover a pant leg hanging out. That's when the attendant has to get a ladder, take out a ceiling tile and unplug the whole row of washers to stop and open your machine. Color me Red. One day I left the laundromat with a basket of wet clothes only to discover I had parked in a handicap space AND my car door would not open. That's when out of the corner of my eye I see a car that looked just like mine two spaces over. There are no words.

I ran into an old friend the other day and we were so happy to see each other. She went on and on about this and that and I am thinking, *who is this person?* I hoped at some point she would say something that jars my memory. She wanted to know if we still lived in the same house and if we had made any changes as she had known the previous owners and had visited there many times. My mind is going a mile a minute as I try to recall who the previous owners were. There has to be a clue in there somewhere. I go on to tell her that we had remodeled and would she like to come over sometime and check it out? A few frantic phone calls and a yearbook hunt and... *of course I knew her.* Oh the stress! Why can't we just say, "sorry, but I don't remember you?" This will never happen, it's like telling someone they have aged so much that no one will ever recognize them again and I am so senile that I don't recognize my own mother. Guess I will fake it as always.

I think everyone has those "hang on to your hair" kind of days. One day the paper shredder only ran backwards, the next day the printer quit working and before the week was over the sewing machine tried to eat my pants. Its things like this that makes life interesting. I am sure as I get older my family will chalk all of this up to the aging process. I hope they remember things really haven't changed that much over the years you just can't out grow ditzy.

I noticed the other day that everyone of importance in my life seems to be younger than I am: my doctor, dentist and even my mailman. Those who were older and wiser are now younger and wiser.

When I was younger if I didn't know the address of a person I might write something like this on the envelope: JOE, ELM STREET, WHITE HOUSE, BLUE SHUTTERS, FRONT PORCH SWING. No problem.

A few months ago I mailed a letter to my granddaughter in Florida. My cousin in Florida called to say she had received it. "That's funny," I said. "Maybe I had the wrong house number. Perhaps she lives on your street." My cousin assured me that if a cute 20-year-old lived in that retirement community they certainly would know about it. She returned the letter and I mailed it again. This time it was returned to me from who-knows-where. I changed the address and sent it out a third time. Now I have over $2.00 in postage and my mail is traveling more than I am.

When my doctor and my dentist retired they had one of their children take over. I love it when the kids go into the family business. They may be meeting me for the first time but I have been hearing about them for years. I sometimes feel it is my duty to let them know exactly how their parents did things. I have retained a treasure trove of information that I can tap into at a moments notice. Things I bet they didn't learn in college.

Sometimes this old world can get pretty hectic so try not to take life too seriously. The lighter side is out there, sometimes you just have to look in the right places.

TRAVEL

Most people like to — or would like to — travel. See the world! But they are usually referring to the destination, not the traveling itself.

"Oh, we had a wonderful time! The island was beautiful. What can I say about the food? Simply delectable."

Then you ask about the trip and that's when the hammer hits reality. The airport was a challenge, the lines were long, and lots of delays. Getting through customs can be tricky, you don't want to look those guys in the eye. One fellow jokingly said he had a lizard in his suitcase and they are still finding his underwear hanging from the rafters. The flight was a roller coaster: at one point my soda flew out of my glass. The cab ride was to die for, and I do mean die for. There was no air conditioning and we hit three chickens and we barely missed a goat.

It was a wonderful trip… we'll never forget it.

Now traveling by car is another rewarding experience if you happen to be the passenger. Sit back, relax and enjoy the scenery. Being the driver is a whole other vacation. A wrong turn can put you in the Chicago Loop at rush hour and Chicago was nowhere near your destination. I understand there are electronic devices that can avert such situations so I printed out my electronically fed instructions. The State of Michigan is surrounded by water and I would think it would be impossible to drive for hours on end and not run into a shore line. I would be wrong. You have the map in your hand but the landscape is starting to repeat itself. My best advice is to toss the map in the dumpster while you are at the gas station getting directions.

I personally like the voice who spoon feeds you as you go: "you will be turning left at the next exit so move into the left turn lane."

Isn't that just precious? She's a good listener, too. I told her my life story and she never said a word. The best traveling companion ever.

How about traveling with children? What a challenge!

"Are we there yet? I need to go to the bathroom. Johnny touched me."

"She said I had cooties."

"Did not!"

"Did so!"

Oh, the joys of the *Family Vacation*. When I was growing up you piled your ten kids in the back seat to go visit friends. With any luck you could get away with leaving one or two behind for a couple of days. This actually happened to my uncle. They had friends over for ice cream and after they had waved their goodbyes they walked into the kitchen to find one left behind in the high chair. There were no cell phones, so the couple got all the way home before they discovered one missing. If I had 10 kids I think it may have taken a couple of days before I realized I was one short.

Another way to travel is the bus tour. How relaxing! Leave the driving to someone else. That's when you discover the entertainment director has a microphone and a career goal of being a standup comedian. For the next 6 hours you don't know whether to choke her or pull the emergency chord.

This is when my daughter has a panic attack and with her nails embedded in my arm, hisses quite loudly, "make her shut up and get me off this bus." I'm thinking a little Xanax may be in order for the ride home.

I never have cared much for flying, which will surprise a lot of people since I have spent most of my life with my head in the clouds. There is just something about having my whole body leave the earth that freaks me out. The first time I flew, the plane circled the airport a couple of times before landing and I was pretty sure the pilot was lost and we would be up there forever. It's not too bad if you can fly nonstop but that is never the case for me. I usually fly into a huge airport where I have to figure out how to get to my next gate which is 500 miles away. When I flew into Key West I had to hop a puddle jumper from Miami. It was raining buckets when the plane landed several feet from the airport. The attendant tossed me an umbrella that I caught in mid-air. Hurricane winds twisted it into a pretzel rendering it totally useless. Did I hear someone yell *run for your life?*

With divine intervention I made it to my gate. I boarded the overly crowded commuter and swore this would be the last time I ever flew again. Of course that was a big fat lie.

When I was a kid, traveling meant getting a dime and riding my bike the one block uptown to hang over a large red cooler full of ice trying to decide what flavor of soda to buy. Those were the days. Today my family will hop on a plane like I hop on the scales and its probably not as scary.

I have traveled a tad over the years but personally I like to sit in my overstuffed rocking chair, get a big bowl of buttered popcorn, a tall glass of soda and turn on the travel channel. See the world from the comfort of your own home. Best of all, the bathroom is just around the corner.

GIFT GIVING

Gift cards seem the way to go today but I still like to see someone open that perfectly wrapped gift that they totally did not expect to get. I love it when they love the gift or at least have to fake a like. The purchasing of such gift should take time and consideration and that is probably why cards are so popular. They are a no-brainer.

Exchanging gifts can be quite the dilemma. What to get? What if the gift you give is cheap but you receive something expensive or you spend a lot of money on someone and they don't give you anything and you say its okay but it's really not? It goes on and on, so when you actually know what a person really wants you will turn the world upside down to get it.

When a friend of mine admired my (after the holiday $1 bargain priced) earmuffs I filed that information under, "I know what she's getting next year for Christmas." Who thought it would take me almost a year before I ran across a pair exactly like mine.

There they were; sitting alone with no tags or price. I latched onto them like glue on felt. The clerk thought they were $10 which I gladly paid. I wrapped them in a pretty blue box and put them under the tree. A few weeks later I slid my hand into my coat pocket to retrieve my ear muffs but they were gone. I looked high and low and traced my thoughts back to when I had last worn them. Oh yea it was that shopping day I found the perfect gift. It got warm and I stuffed them in my coat pocket. No, it couldn't be, did they fall out of my pocket? Did I actually purchase my own ear muffs? Did I actually pay $10 for something I already owned? I ripped the box open, put them on my head and took a long walk. Candles are always a good idea.

My husband and I gave up gift giving years ago. He could not keep a secret. He would let the cat out of the bag without even knowing it. One conversation went something like this: "I had to return your gift, it was the same color sweater my mother is getting you." Really, what color is that?

Once when I asked him if he had seen a little brown box I needed for a gift he said "oh yes, I wrapped your socks in it." Socks, huh, I can hardly wait. He never could find the right size box for his gifts leaving me to assume that huge box under the tree with my name on it must be that expensive electric fry pan I had been wanting. Wow I don't think I spent enough on him. Best go shopping for more. Not knowing what is going on he goes shopping to even things out. This can go on right up until they place the closed sign in the store window on Christmas day.

Over the years our family has grown and Christmas gift giving has taken on a whole new meaning. We have tried several things. One year I filled stockings for everyone and that proved to be more expensive than getting them a gift. Then there was the year we all brought a gender appropriate gift. If you were a girl, you brought a girls gift and so on. Sounded good in theory until my 12 year old grandson walked off with a bottle of vodka.

Drawing names seemed like a good idea. We set a limit of $20 per gift. It seemed simple enough except my son-in-law didn't pay attention and showed up with a $100 dollar gift. Dang, I wish he had gotten my name.

One year we thought it would be fun to do an old fashion Christmas and make our gift. I enthusiastically got out my power tools and made outside flower boxes for the girls and 4-foot by 8-foot fishing rod holders for the guys out of ¾ inch plywood. I had to have help getting them out of the basement. We all got some pretty neat gifts that year but this was way too time consuming.

We have decided it's not the gift, it's the fun of being together, reminiscing, making memories and yes you can always plan on some laughs along the way.

My husband and I came up with the perfect way to celebrate special occasions. On our anniversary, for instance, we would go to the card shop and pick out the biggest and most expensive cards, exchange them in the store, read them and put them back on the shelf and with any luck we will have a coupon to the sub shop.

Buying gifts for non-family-members can be a challenge. That's when you need to find the perfect gift that no one could have possibly thought of.

One word comes to mind. *Regift.* Remember that hideous orange bowl with the blue fish that you declared to be gorgeous at your wedding shower? Perhaps it's time to dust it off and give it to someone who will really appreciate it.

Now this can be tricky and should only be done if there is a state line involved and even then, you take the chance of someone remembering this most unforgettable gift so be ready with "I loved mine so much I wanted you to have one just like it." Fake a headache and leave, ending any more discussion.

What on earth do you get the elderly? After so many years there is nothing left that they don't already have. They could never use up those endless bottles of lotion, and they have enough coffee mugs to use a different one every day of the year. You have another problem if they have downsized and have a limited space. Countertop appliances are out of the question. When I reach that time in my life I hope my gifts are limited to candy or flowers. You can eat one and the other will die.

I always liked getting gifts from my children, particularly those little homemade cards that say, I love you mommy, you are the best mommy ever, you are so beautiful. Save those, you may need them later. Two of my young children got me the best birthday gift ever. It was a hand painted porcelain bell which read, *Happy 25th Anniversary*. That one is a keeper for sure.

I don't think we ever outgrow the thrill of having someone hand us a brightly wrapped present with a beautiful bow. Everyone loves a surprise no matter how old we get. It has been said that it's the thought that counts, not the gift. Truth be known, while I appreciate the thought, this does not get you off the hook.

I want presents.

SURGERY

Now, there are times when I am not always happy with the shape of my body, but I am very fond of my body parts and hope to leave this world with as many of them intact as I can. That's probably why I had my tonsils out twice. Just didn't want to part with them.

The one time I did need major surgery my husband spent the whole time in the ER scoping out an accident that was far more interesting. It took a while to hunt him down. I realized he probably would not be the best person to depend on in a crisis. I was happy my mother was around to keep things moving along.

In later years I was blessed with two daughters who would be willing to drop everything to hold my hand and see me through my times of pain and agony. They'd also keep a close watch on dad. Sometimes

I think they are a bit eager for such opportunities.

A few years ago I needed a cornea transplant. What on earth is a cornea? I was told it is like the crystal on your watch, kind of holds everything in place.

You remember those goofy glasses where the eyeball bounces in and out on a spring? Guess they don't have a cornea.

I wondered if this donated cornea might come in colors. Maybe I could get a pair to match the one black and one brown shoe I wore last week? Maybe this donor had a special talent that could be passed on to me. Perhaps he or she played the bagpipes. I always wanted to play the bagpipes. There is always the chance that I could reject this cornea. In that case there may be a parrot and a patch in my future.

The day of surgery my daughters were there to cheer me on. I think the word went out something like this: "Hey, let's see if we can get a couple of days off. Mom's going under the knife. It'll be a blast!"

While they stood vigil I was introduced to twilight sleep; in other words I was drunk out of my mind and became a babbling brook of useless information. I don't even want to think of the cats I may have let out of the bag that day. After surgery they tell me I wolfed down a turkey sandwich and I don't even like turkey.

With one eye stitched shut my darling daughters led me to my room where I mistook the closet for a bathroom and brushed my teeth with a tube of hand cream.

The next day I apologized to the surgeon for my ramblings and explained that he could have put me into a deeper sleep at any time. He replied I was far too entertaining for that. Then he asked if I would like to see the pictures.

I said, "Pictures? I knew we were having a good time but I didn't know anyone took pictures."

That's when he pulled out the pictures of my eye from before and after surgery.

A week later: "Mom's getting her stitches out. Let's get a room with a pool and bring the kids!"

What would I do without them?.

That transplant was a blessing and I will forever be grateful to the donor. As the years have passed that eye has lost some vision, so it has become my bad eye. Well, that leaves the other one to be known as the good eye. Good eye sort of leads bad eye around but together they work quite well.

One day good eye became ill and there was nothing bad eye could do to help. That is when I consulted the pros to see if they could get good eye back on track.

My daughter Robbin drew the short straw, so she took me to the Eye Institute. After I saw the doctor, Robbin directed me to the restroom while she made the next appointment. I entered the little restroom at the end of the hall and headed straight to the handicap stall. Hearing someone else enter prompted me to peer under the door. Wow, that gal sure has big feet and I wonder why she is facing the wall. Then I hear what I think is water running. You have to be kidding. That's when I realize I just may not be in the ladies room after all. I have no alternative but to hold my breath and pray the other person will finish up and get out of there. When I am pretty sure it is safe I met up with Robbin who was at the end of the hall impatiently tapping her foot.

"What took you so long? I have been waiting forever," she said.

"I was in the wrong restroom."

"You were where? Didn't you see the little icon above the door?"

Really, if I could see I wouldn't be here in the first place. They need to paint a life size picture on the front of that door. That was my excuse that day, but this was not my first rodeo. I never pay attention and have ended up in the wrong restroom several times. Usually the urinal is my first clue that I have run amok and I make a quick exit.

On our return visit, the eye test was not so good. As Robbin and I were waiting to see the Doctor, things were a little tense but not for long. As we sat there Robbin tells me there may be some good news and some bad news. Bad news is I may be going blind. Good news: I may be getting a dog. You just can't make stuff like this up.

As it turns out she was wrong on both counts and with medication and some minor surgery all is well for now. I am sure if things go awry they will all be there to cheer me on because we are family and that's what we do.

When I had my nose surgery, my girls came through for me as usual. They stood by my bed as the drugs were taking effect. And as I was being wheeled away and muttering incoherently I heard Jeana say, "What did mom say?"

Robbin replied, "I think she said she loves me best."

This surgery took place on a top floor of a beautiful hotel. Just when you think you know what goes on up there, you really do not have a clue. You go in frumpy and come out fabulous. Well let's just say the fabulous part comes later, Right after surgery it's more like frightful or freaky. No, you won't be leaving by the front door anytime soon. There is a special exit for you, one that leads down a dark hallway and into the alley where your daughters are waiting to whisk you away to a celebration. A celebration that involves a Mr. Potato Head cake, a flashing Rudolph nose and a card signed Cyrano de

Bergerac.

I'm sure, someday when I have the big one they will be there in their jester suits to keep me laughing to the bitter end.

I don't mind seeing my doctor as long as it is at the grocery store or church, and if I go to the hospital I want to be the visitor and not the detainee. Don't count on it as there are always those unexpected incidents that can flip your life like a three legged stool.

One minute you're getting out of the car and the next minute you are getting back in with a broken ankle. In these times you really appreciate the comforting words of your mate. Words like "Oh my God, get in the car. Look at the size of that ankle! What are we going to do? Where should we go?" He continues with "surgery? Oh yes, I see… Surgery! That thing is huge."

Well that made me feel a lot better. If he hadn't been driving 100 MPH I would have slapped him silly. This is when you are really, really happy to see the ER door. A little valium for the driver and a cast for me, thank you very much.

I hope as I get older that my medical-care-people have a good sense of humor. With this family they will need one.

HOUSEKEEPING AND HOME APPLIANCES

My mother was the queen of housework. I think dirt was scared to death of her. You would think a little of that could have came my way, but it was not to be. I would like to blame her in some way but alas: I am of my own making.

Mother washed the ceilings in her closet. What could possibly go on in a closet that would render the ceilings dirty? If there is such an activity I'm sure I don't want to know about it. Up until she told me this I didn't even know closets had ceilings.

I remember the day my dentist recalled my father telling him that my mother had washed his tooth brush with soap. He blew bubbles for weeks.

Her basement and garage were spotless. I

have a spider gala going on in mine. They really are great weavers. Mother insisted that every week all of the knick knacks were marched to the kitchen sink to be submerged in hot sudsy water to be properly scrubbed. I have no idea what they did all week to deserve such a ritual.

The story that will forever be engraved on our brains occurred when she extended her expertise to the family car. My two young children waited with wide eyes as grandma came toward the car with their ice cream cones, now imagine the horror as grandma smashed them into the car window because it was so clean she didn't know it was rolled up. Of course the rest of us could hardly come up for air as we rolled out of the car screaming with laughter.

Housework is not my forte. I have my limits. When polishing the floors, I usually hang the caution tape as a reminder that running around the house in my stocking feet may give me the ability to do a triple back flip, the outcome of which is never good.

I hate to dust. It makes me sneeze. We

used to call those cute little particles sunbeams. We even sang songs about them. Turns out they are ugly little critters that when left undisturbed can devour large quantities of linens. Did we really need to know this? You can't get rid of dust. Those little mites multiply faster than rabbits. My solution, set fire to the feather dusters and stop knocking yourself out.

We all have a house full of home appliances. It seems an appliance is a piece of equipment or device designed for a particular use. I wonder sometimes if my appliances know this. Oh, I do my best to guide them down the right path, but sometimes they have a mind of their own. If you look the other way my hand mixer has the ability to hurl dough six foot into the air while it eats my shirt. My coffee maker demands a new filter every time I use it or it spews out ugly green swill. I gave up on the electric knife and now use it to trim the hedges, and the steam iron scares me.

The garbage disposal sounded like it was eating ground glass and the dishes in the dishwasher came out with more food on them than when they went in. Who's living in there anyway? I had them both removed. Dishcloth looks at me crosswise and I toss it.

The upright vacuum is a regular diva. A gentle tug of the cord and she does a semi-twirl and passes out cold. The canister has a mind of its own. The other day I went from one room to another and it held on to the doorway like we were going to the death chambers. It flung itself upside down, activating the cord release bar which in turn caused the plug to come out of the wall at the speed of sound and hit me in the head. I put in wood floors.

What is up with the refrigerator? It has more moans and groans than a cat caught in a screen door. Someone could actually be breaking into my house with a sledge hammer and I would probably say, "Oh, it's just the refrigerator." There have been times when that thought has brought me great comfort. Last winter I thought the old girl was on the blink so I loaded everything into the trunk of my car. It was a little inconvenient standing out there in my pajamas, drinking juice from the carton, you know, frostbite and all. Three days later I discovered there was nothing wrong with the refrigerator so I lugged everything back into the house. My neighbors should sell tickets.

Remember when you sent the kids and pets to grandmas so you could don the hazard uniform, goggles and all, just to clean the oven? If a drop of this stuff should hit the floor you could see all the way to your basement. Welcome to the present. My new and improved oven is amazing. You lock the door and the heat goes up so high you can bend steel. I think there is a little suicidal guy in there ready to sacrifice it all just to keep my oven spotless. Once the door is open, there lies his little pile of ashes. I sweep them into a ceremonial box, say a prayer and put them in the trash.

Now how hard is it to change the sheets on a bed? You take the soiled ones off, toss them in the washer, and replace them with the clean ones. It's not rocket science. That's why you can imagine the look on my face when I opened the dryer to discover I was missing one queen size sheet. Now that's impossible. This happens with socks all of the time but I have never, ever, lost a whole sheet. That is not a small item. I searched that house up and down and then did what I quite often do, retraced my steps. There it was under the clean sheet. I had actually put the clean sheet right on top of the dirty one. Maybe there's a chance I might relocate those lost socks after all.

We've come a long way from bashing our belongings on the old river rock.

There was the knuckle busting washboard, then the ringer washer. The safety police would have had a heyday with that. One wrong move and your arm could be as flat as a stick of gum. Well, today we have been blessed with the automatic washing machine. Nothing is better than hearing your clothes being swished back and forth in a sea of soapy water. Don't get too comfortable: that thing has a dark side. It can become unbalanced and pitch a real fit. The next thing you know it is walking towards you. Perhaps it is time to look for a replacement or call the local appliance repair man. Nice, friendly guy. The last time I had the pleasure of his company it only cost me $60 to discover I didn't have the dryer plugged in properly.

I hate paying for water and air. I heard a kid ask, "what is that thing on top of the sink?" I said it was a faucet and water came out of it. " Hmm", he said, "where's the cap?"

I am way too old for this, so you can see how irritating it is for me to pay for airwaves. The cable company tells you one price and in a year you are taking a second mortgage on the house just to be able to have access to 100 channels and you only watch 2. Tried spending my summers without paying and ended up hanging out the window with a bent coat hanger in each hand and my head wrapped in aluminum foil. That's when I decided I would just spend my summers watching movies. So far I have about 200 chick flicks. Let me see, at $5 a movie that's about a total of $1,000. Boy did I show those cable guys. I wonder what I did with my radio...

Now we come to the "Bent Handled

Snow Shovel." Those of you who know me have heard me speak of my beloved shovel many times over the years. Pure genius, a shovel that bends so you don't have too. I was so excited about mine I bought my 80 year old mother one. Some people just don't appreciate the finer things in life, so now I own two. I have to get up mighty early on a snowy day to stand guard with my bent handled shovels just in case some crazy guy with a snow blower should decide to do me a favor. The shovels hang side by side on the garage wall all polished and ready for that next winter blast. I visit them every now and then and dream of the days when that white stuff falls from the sky.

Raking leaves on a windy day can be a challenge. You can scream, jump up and down, stomp on the rake, throw yourself on the ground and froth at the mouth to no avail. It's hopeless, but on a good day there is nothing like the "Over the Shoulder Leaf Blower." This apparatus does not just go over your shoulder, it goes over your head. Of course I have two of them. They hang side by side on the garage wall right next to my "Bent Handled Snow Shovels."

Most of my yard tools hang on hooks on the garage wall. I say most because I hardly ever put things back where they belong. When I went to get the rake I was surprised to find it hanging right where it should be. In my eagerness to retrieve the rake I neglected to see the pitchfork hanging right below so I was totally unprepared for what happened next.

As I pulled on the rake the pitchfork flew off its hook and stabbed me in the foot. Are you kidding me? I looked down and saw my foot nailed to the floor. I was overcome with a wave of panic. I had to pull that tine out. I was pretty sure this action would result in me fainting or throwing up. To my surprise I did neither. Man, I really am brave.

With blood spurting out the top of my foot, I hobbled into the cottage and put my plan into action. First, wash the wound. Second, apply a little antiseptic cream and a band aid. That should do it. By now you should have figured out that I am not a nurse. Lucky for me my neighbor was but why bother her as I had everything under control? Call me Florence Nightingale.

The next morning the foot was red and swollen and I couldn't move it so I'm thinking maybe — just maybe — I have broken a few bones. Funny, the thought of infection never entered my mind. I had taken all of the precautions hadn't I? Perhaps it was time to consult my neighbor and friend: the nurse. She rolled her eyes as I explained the events of the previous day and my uneducated conclusion. Before I knew it, she and another crazy friend loaded me in the car and headed to the hospital. They dropped me off with well wishes assuring me they would return right after they had lunch. How lucky am I to have such good friends?

As I hobbled into the hospital I was wondering how serious could a puncture wound be? It seems it was serious enough to merit an x-ray, a foot wash, a tetanus shot and an antibiotic IV. After a hour I called my friends to retrieve me. When they pulled into the parking lot I was sitting on the curb holding a big white bag and my foot was wrapped from my knee to my toes in a sterile white bandage. They drove right by. Really, how could they not see me? They said, "Oh we saw you." Priceless!

The very next summer my kitchen shears came apart and one half stabbed my other foot and a few weeks prior I dropped a tool and broke my toe. Unbelievable! My friends, I wear a size 5 shoe. Not a big target. I am thinking with an aim like that I should probably take up darts but I am sure I would most likely drop one. I guess we all know the rest of that story.

Life can be a challenge at times. I guess the best thing to do is find the lighter side of an event and go with it. When we can laugh at ourselves and our inadequacies we find life really can be a bowl of cherries, pits and all!

SHOPPING

I love to shop. There is nothing better than spending a day with a friend looking for a bargain. The only thing that can ruin a good shopping day is having a plan. Looking for that one particular item — which you are never going to find— is a real downer. Someone asked me what I was shopping for; I told her I will know it when I see it. My eyes are focused on the big red 80% sales rack and there it will be.

Over the years my insecurities have led me to shop for previously owned items. I figure if someone else liked it that's good enough for me. Of course I seem to forget they didn't like it well enough to keep it. Garage sales are the way to go. You never know what you will run across. Case in point: those tin mushroom lights for my garden path. Now every night I can go out in my pajamas and plug them in so I can sit at the window and look at them. Special!

When it comes to garage sales you might say my friend Barb and I are the dynamic duo. Years ago we met a couple having a yard sale and before we left we had toured their flower gardens, looked through their *Trip to China* album, signed their guest book and were invited back for dinner. Out of curiosity our husbands agreed to go. They had a lovely home way back into the woods a considerable distance from the main road. Anything could go on back there. We really knew nothing about these people. They could be part of a cult or even worse we could end up having to buy some waterless cookware. Not to worry. The table was beautiful with a linen table cloth and napkins. The dinner was delicious and ended with a big slab of homemade pie. We have formed a close friendship with these guys and when someone asks us where we met them we always say we got them at a garage sale. Best deal ever.

One day after following the balloons on a mailbox Barb and I thought we had hit the best sale ever. They had hung decorations and were serving food. There was even a nice cake for dessert. What a unique idea. A nice gentleman even came over to help us open our car door. It seemed we were the first to arrive. Turns out we had just crashed a family reunion. We all had a good laugh. We told the gentleman we were the entertainment committee and he invited us to stay saying no one knows any one at these things anyway. We were tempted but declined.

I spotted a fake palm tree at a church rummage sale and I was not a bit surprised when Barb loaded it into my car. Every garden should have a palm tree and I will admit it looks pretty cool in hers. Do we really need this stuff? Of course not, but the fun is in the hunt and a day spent with a good friend.

Sometimes one just gets caught up in the moment when they are having a sale. A friend of mine sold her two daughter's bikes and shoes while they were in the house having a snack and before the day was over she had sold the family car. That spring she dragged the living room furniture out onto the lawn to do some serious cleaning and you can imagine how that ended. People will buy and sell just about anything. Everything has a price.

One can get so wrapped up in these sales that they can inadvertently forget where the car is and get into someone's auto other than their own. This has happened to me several times. The last time I got into a red van and said, "who bought an infant car seat?' While amusing, most of my friends don't seem surprised.

You can meet all kinds of people at these sales. There is the antique dealer who rises early, dons her helmet and roller blades, places a magnifying glass in her shirt pocket and wraps a plastic measuring tape around her neck. The sale starts at eight but she's there by seven. When the garage door goes up she's out of the gate like a race horse. She goes directly to the English bone china plate and says to the owner, "Five dollars! would you take $2? And could you wrap it?"

Next we have the elderly couple with the sticker in the back window, THIS CAR STOPS AT ALL GARAGE SALES. What it really means is, they may stop in the middle of the road for no reason and if you hit them, you will probably be sent to jail by the AARP.

Then there is the lady in the pink floppy hat with the round green sticker from the last sale. She is there to see what you are buying. Once she sees your eyes zero in on an item she will climb over ten people — small children included — to get it first and then claim she had been looking for that item all day. Sure you have.

What's up with the drive by? You have worked for weeks digging out your lifelong treasures, pricing every item with stickers that never stay stuck, and making sure your displays are enticing enough to lure in the most unexpected buyer. It usually rains that day and it is 100 degrees in the shade. Not to worry as you sit under your big striped umbrella with anticipation of that first big sale. Sure enough, here comes a rusty blue van. It slows down and heads pop out of the windows, surveying your wares. Maybe they will take it all and you can afford that dream vacation. Then the unthinkable happens, the van speeds up and you can barley see the bumper sticker that reads EAT MY DUST. What about that dream vacation? Well that goes to the dealer with the bone china plate.

We have so many options now. The dollar stores seem to be quite popular. I feel if I am only spending a dollar per item I should get one of everything. It is amazing how fast those dollars add up. Most likely half of those items will eventually find a spot in your next yard sale and with any luck you might net 25 cents per item. Don't count on it.

THE FAMILY
WITH CHILDREN

I got lucky. I have three of the most awesome kids ever. I know having me for a mom couldn't have been easy for them but they survived. They all have children of their own now and so they must realize how it was for me. Parenting is a "Learn as you go, on the job training" process. One day you are out and about without a care in the world and the next you are holding this infant boy child that is depending on you for everything and you are saying to yourself *Good Lord, what have we done? That's it, this will be our only child and I will be lucky if he survives* and then 2 ½ years later you do it all over again. It's a girl, wow, that's a family! But you are only 23 and as the years go by you start getting the "baby" itch and 8 ½ years later, it's another girl. Turn around twice and your son is graduating high school the same week your daughter is graduating kindergarten.

You enroll your first child in everything: little league, swim lessons, Scouts... Randy was a Cub Scout, I was the den mother. He made a pine wood derby car, I made a pine wood derby car. His fell to pieces and I prayed mine would too. No problem, I still have my furry little cross-eyed trophy that reads NO ONE IS PERFECT.

My daughter Robbin was 8 when I took her to the pharmacy with me. From there I went on to the grocery store and then home. My husband was eating lunch and I nonchalantly asked him if he had fixed Robbin some lunch. The expression on his face was pure horror as he blurted out, "Good Lord, have you taken leave of your senses? You took her with you!"

That's when I discovered I had the ability to drive 100 MPH, laugh hysterically, sob uncontrollably, and wet my pants all at the same time. There she was, right where I had left her: at the pharmacy looking at the toys. There's a lifetime of therapy for both of us.

What was I thinking?

A few years later we stopped at a rest area and one of her friends asked "What would happen if your parents forgot and left us here?"

Robbin replied "It's already been done."

I blame it on the fact that I was pregnant with my late-in-life child. I was 30.

Since then I have not lost any of my children. I did however go to pick my son up after a week at camp and made a perfect fool of myself yelling "WHAT HAVE YOU DONE WITH MY CHILD?" only to discover I was at the wrong camp.

Gee, I thought he was there all week and it turns out he was at another camp. Go figure.

By the time my third child came along I had an 11 year old and an 8 year old to help me keep track of her. Parenting is not for the weak of heart!

My third child Jeana called the other day to ask if she ever had chickenpox. I really couldn't remember. I'm sure I had some sort of record of those things but where they were was beyond me. I told her to call her sister. That's one advantage of having older children.

Jeana suggested maybe I should check her baby book. Hmm, I meant to get one of those. Now I am feeling like a real loser in the mom department and the next time I go to the store I am going to pick one up for both the girls. They are in their 40s and 50s now and I won't live forever.

On my behalf, I had a beautiful book for my first born. It went up to age 90. I would have to live to be 110 to finish it so I gave it to him when he was 50. He has no idea where it is.

Who doesn't love grandchildren? I have been blessed with 7 of them. After all the craziness of raising my own kids they still have the confidence in me to babysit the grandkids from time to time. Now, *there* is a whole other book.

Maybe someday I will be blessed with great grandchildren and I hope all of them will have the ability to see the funnier side of life.

Do I give my kids and grandkids advice? Are you kidding me? I haven't figured it all out yet. Hopefully they will be able to teach me something. Thanks guys, for keeping my spirits up and making my life way more worthwhile.

I love them and best of all I think they kind of like me.

DIET (JUST ANOTHER FOUR LETTER WORD)

I t is rare these days to have a conversation with anyone that does not eventually turn into a discussion about diet, weight, looks and how much water you drink per day, and how many steps you take, and so on. Here is some of the wisdom I have acquired over the years. Believe me: my track record leaves a lot to be desired.

Diet is the most understood word in the universe. The word "diet" means foodstuff, edibles, provisions, nutriment, fare, rations. So, I guess the word diet depicts all of us, but usually when we use the word diet we really mean "I'm a big fat pig and I need to go on a diet to not be a big fat pig."

Well we are in luck. It seems there are groves of people who know just exactly how to do that. They can tell you what to eat, how to eat, when to eat, and how much to eat. Everyone has an idea, a club, a program, and an unsolicited opinion. What's your size, your number, your goal?

Every magazine, talk show host, and cooking show has something to say. It just goes on and on. I will admit over a period of years I have been known to battle the bulge. I blame this on my mother. I was born in the 40s when a nice plump, rosy cheeked baby was a sign of good parenting. My brother and I were just the opposite, therefore we became the recipients of a thick brown syrup which I believe laid dormant for about 30 years. You just can't fight a beast like that.

In the 60s, 70s and 80s, I tried some pretty crazy things. Did they work? Well here is where the waters got muddy for me as my attention span is limited. I have a hard time with self discipline, but those years make for some pretty interesting stories.

I remember the water diet. All that water

was just going to flush all those extra pounds right down the porcelain pit. This is probably a good time to think about updating that reading material in the bathroom, and best not be planning any long trips for a while. Sounded crazy at the time but as the years pass it turns out water is good for you. I don't know if it flushes fat but it seems everyone is carrying around a bottle of the good stuff. People can't get through an hour long church service without a bottle tucked between the hymnal and prayer book. There are contests to see who can put away the most gallons in a day. This is one of my unsolicited opinions but I think your bladder can hold just so much and your kidneys did not come with a life time warranty. Keep them on overtime and they will scream for an early retirement. When that day comes you won't be shopping in the big girl's panty department any more; you will be getting your undies in the pharmacy department. Yikes! When it comes to liquid consumption I think I will stick to moderation. So this may not be the best way to lose weight for me. I kind of like shopping in the big girl's department.

In the 70s we were all introduced to the grapefruit diet. Just eat one half of this acidic fruit before each meal and the acid was going to eat away your fat like a beaver gnawing on a tree branch. Putting a section of this fruit in my mouth was right up there with watching someone suck a lemon. Maybe with a few pounds of sugar sprinkled on top but I sort of think this would defeat my purpose. My husband Dale just rolled his eyes as he watched me stock the basement shelves with large bags of grapefruit. This program was doomed to fail from the get go. I had absolutely no idea that fresh fruit had such a short shelf life. I had a sale in my basement but this stuff can get fuzzy real fast. Well, I gave it my best. It makes me feel good to know I am contributing to the garbage man's job security.

I liked counting calories. One of the perks is there is quite a large margin for error. Calorie counting can be a little iffy. Is the measuring cup suppose to be level, heaped or pressure packed? Hmm, I think I will opt for overflowing, or maybe I will just eyeball it. I have always been good at guessing things, that's why I have all of those "maybe someday" clothes in the closet.

I loved the diet club. I made so many friends they made me president. Boy, could I tell those gals how to lose weight! To set a good example I would ride my bike three miles to the meetings. I was good at this. One gal lost over 100 pounds. Oh, if I could have just practiced what I preached. Little did they know that after the meeting and everyone had gone home I rode right up to the corner store to get my candy bar fix. I told myself it was a hard job being the president of a club and besides I needed that extra energy to pedal that two-wheeler home. On a day I thought I had gained weight I would wear my heavy clothes and a long wig that felt like it weighed at least a couple of pounds. Let's make this gain a big one so the next week I only had to ditch the heavy clothes and the wig and *voila!* Automatic weight loss. Eventually it all caught up with me. I really liked that club and I really miss those girls.

If I ever come back in a second life I think I would like to reincarnate as a bear. What a life! You only have to work the summer months and your job is to frolic around in the sun all day and try to eat as much as possible. When the cold snowy months of winter arrive, you just crawl into a nice homey warm cave and sleep until your alarm goes off. You won't believe this but you come out of that cave looking like a million bucks, nice and trim! And if you are a female you just might find you gave birth and you didn't even know it. Believe me that will never happen with a human. Never. Of course I don't know if I could deal with that heavy fur coat during those long hot days but I guess the word here is compromise.

As far as food goes I prefer my fruit in a pie and my beans baked with bacon and brown sugar, and while we are on the subject of brown sugar: when did they get rid of the lumps? I loved popping those little hard balls into my mouth. Now I have to eat out of the bag with a spoon. When my sweet tooth really gets the best of me I like to take a hit off of the Maple Syrup bottle. Make no mistake, I mean Pure Maple Syrup. None of that cheap imitation stuff for me.

Exercise is always good no matter what you are putting into your mouth. Keeps the blood flowing and the mind sharp and with a little effort you may burn off a few of those calories. Of course, let's not get too crazy here. I think we all have that one friend who leaps out of bed into the middle of the gym, and sweats for a couple of hours before jogging 20 miles home all before breakfast, which consists of protein powder and freshly mown grass. On the other hand I do hope she is around if I ever have to be rescued from a burning building.

I prefer a simpler routine such as walking. A much gentler pace and a good idea except for that embarrassing trip and fall. First you are up and then bam! you are kissing the sidewalk and you're thinking, "am I hurt?" And then your next thought is, "did anyone see me?" That's when you usually hear this voice coming from far above you asking if you are okay. I don't care if I were bleeding internally I would not admit it. "Nope, just checking out this crack here, boy someone should do something about this. Thanks for asking." You wait until you are pretty sure the well-wisher is gone and you crawl home on your hands and knees.

I also like to ride my bike. I don't like helmets but on the other hand I don't like open head injuries either so it's a toss up. I usually opt for the helmet. I load the bike up with snacks, water bottle, mosquito spray, pepper spray (you know, for the grizzly bears) and head down the old bike trail keeping an eye out for low flying pigeons. You might eat a few bugs along the way but what the heck? One year during the winter months I bought one of those things you set your bike in so you can ride it in the kitchen. Do you know how many minutes there are in a half hour? More than you'd think. Boring! Sorry to say but that little bike thing went to the gadget graveyard with all of the other exercise equipment.

My brother says his waist is bigger than his inseam so now he thinks he is taller lying down than he is standing. It really doesn't matter to me. I'm short and square. I am probably the same standing, sitting or lying down.

I have heard some refer to their body shape as an apple or a pear. Give me a break. If I had to describe my shape as something other than human, I guess I would be a short tree. I have pretty good limbs but my trunk is a bit on the bulky side. Dressing me is like tossing a camouflage quilt over a rain barrel. Khaki and tacky is how I roll. This tree likes to blend in with the forest.

When it comes to health and exercise, my kids have it all figured out. They and their families run marathons, ride bikes from one end of the state to the other, join gyms and have personal trainers. They eat healthy (well most of the time). They have gadgets that tell them how many calories they burn, how many steps they take and everything one would want to know about their bodies and then some. I think I may have to take up a few more bad habits just to get that family tree to bend a bit more my way. I just hope there wasn't a mix up at the hospital and some Olympic athlete is wondering why their offspring is a couch potato. I really am proud of them and the best thing is they don't preach to me about my haphazard habits. They all look wonderful and they have persuaded me to think about some lifestyle changes. If all else fails, it is reassuring to know they will be strong enough to get me out of the bathtub in my old age.

When they lay me out in the end I would prefer to go in my nice fluffy white, zip-up-the-front bathrobe. Maybe I should be looking for a new one since there's a chance I may outlive this one. If anyone picks out a pastel coffin for me I will haunt them to the end. I have been thinking about that display of photos. Maybe I should get some professional shots taken just in case. I hear they can take off a few pounds and inches if you want. See it all works out in the end. Not that I plan to go anytime soon but a gal needs to be prepared.

FURRY FAMILY FRIENDS

We had a miniature collie when I was a kid, as wide as she was tall. She was a great dog. She ate table scraps out of a blue tin coffee can. She never gave us a day's grief and we loved her. Over the years I have discovered just what a diamond in the rough she really was. We have had seven dogs, two hamsters, a Camilla (depending on how long they live this one has been traveling incognito in a basement of a house we haven't lived in for thirty years), one cat, one turtle and a bird. Easiest pet ever was the bird. It went to bed when told, could be left alone and ate like a bird and in the end he could be buried in a snack size baggie.

Remember the little painted-back turtles purchased at the five and dime? Mine came with a small kidney shaped dish with a plastic palm tree in the middle. That turtle amused me for a long time and when his life on earth was over we flushed him in the toilet where the goldfish had gone the week before. Today you can easier adopt a child from a foreign country than purchase a turtle. First the questionnaire, what is the turtle being used for? Are you going to eat him? Will he be exposed to children, etc.? Then comes the identification, I gave them my passport. The cost will be ten times that of his painted ancestor, but it's all worth it when you see him float around in his big aquarium with all the colored stones and turtle toys. Then one day you are cleaning the tank and some of those beautiful stones fall into the garbage disposal. Whoops! Two days after the new disposal is installed the turtle goes bottom up.

I had a wonderful grandmother who would take our dogs when they didn't quite work out, and most of them did not. The Springer Spaniel was a jumping bean and could land in the middle of the table with just one bounce. The little Rat Terrier spent most of his life trying to escape over the back yard fence after being struck with a golf ball. The Poodle jumped off the bed and broke her leg. They all had their little quirks and ended up at grandmas. The best dog ever was the one my daughter, Robbin, dropped on us. Its father had definitely been a traveling salesman. She was a small pointed nose mongrel and my daughter named her Asti. She looked less like champagne and more like a really bad bottle of beer. Robbin was going to take her back right after she graduated college, then right after she got married, and then right after they got a house... so we had Asti for many years. The day came when Robbin took her home and that Christmas someone left a box of candy under the tree. Asti finally proved worthy of her name as she died eating a box of Godiva Chocolates.

Up until the time we got Bailey we had never had a cat and never wanted one. My daughter Jeana dropped him off. We gave ourselves one week to find him a home and ended up having him for fifteen years. This was a Gestapo Cat. He was big and intimidating. He hated to travel and hid if he even saw a suitcase. He didn't like other cars to pass us on the highway so once he was in the vehicle the race was on. Funny thing, he did like to get in the neighbors van every time they opened the door. Guess he knew there was not as much chance as a snowball in hell that they would ever take him anywhere. Even though he was loud and demanding and I complained about him daily I'd take him back in a flash. I really miss that old ball of fur.

When my grandsons were little my daughter, unbeknown to the family, rescued Jack. It had been years since the Asti incident and she thought the boys should have a pet. She was looking for a kitten and found a large black mix in need of a good home. She tied a rope around him and headed to the local pet store and $100 later had the necessary supplies. The boys were delighted when they saw Jack. That night, while Robbin was out my son-in-law David returned from work, saw the dog and assumed he belonged to the babysitter. Surprise, Surprise!

Being in the navy for 20 years pretty much kept my son Randy pet free but my daughter Jeana made up for that. Cooper was a big gentle Chocolate Lab. who was ravenous twenty-four/seven. In the years I knew him he ate a tray of jalapeño peppers, a pan of brownies and three pounds of ground beef. On Thanksgiving Day one of the neighbors called to ask if Cooper had been in their garage. It seems they were missing a thanksgiving turkey and a pot of pulled pork. There was no denying that he was the thief as part of the carcass was discovered in the back yard. Busted!

Our neighbors had one of those large red hound dogs. He had a gentle soul but suffered from separation anxiety. Every time his owners left he would howl for hours on end. After a day away I went over to inform them we had a family outdoor barbecue and their dog howled the whole day. The reply was, "I'm sure he did." Really, that's it, that's all you've got? I am starting to wonder if I crept out in the dead of night and buried bacon grease in their yard if this gentle giant could actually dig his way to China.

I like pets — I really do — but I like them better when they belong to someone else so they can do their duty in their yard and not mine. When they do it in mine I will no doubt step in it five times. Fall is the worst. Huge piles of doggie doo can be under those leaves. Before you can even smell it, you are in it.

It would be nice to have a second heartbeat in the house but let's face it: I am way too immature to take on that type of responsibility. I had a hard enough time keeping track of my children.

SINGLE AND SEVENTY

When I made that u-turn from the 60s to 70s I had been single for 5 years. What to do, what to do? Being married from the time I was 18 gave me very little experience in the single world. Seems some family members think I should be dating; isn't that a hoot? I think you actually have to have a living breathing body for that. Now where would I find one of those? Even if I found one, think of the stress. What if he asked me out to dinner? Where would we go? What on earth would I wear? And then there's that what to order thing. I'd have to check out the restaurant a week before to see what's on the menu.

What if I liked him and he didn't like me? Or even worse, what if he liked me and I didn't like him? I can't even return a rotting head of lettuce; how on earth could I handle a situation like that? I would probably be stuck with him for all of eternity.

Where to find someone in your 70s? How about the internet? Think of the look on my face when a cow is delivered to my door and I thought I was setting up a date with a farmer. Way too risky for me.

I love it when your best friends get involved. You know the couple who would do anything for you. They ask you to go to the movies with them and when they open the car door for you, wham! Blind sided. There sits a guy you have never laid eyes on before. He could be a serial killer for all you know. They introduce him to you as their first cousins second ex-husband. Good Lord! He seems nice until he begins to tell you all about his bad knees, weak heart and he has no idea what that rash is. You are thinking you will never forgive those do-good friends. This guy is looking for a nurse and a purse. Well I am pretty safe on both counts. I have no money and the sight of blood makes me vomit.

I struck up a conversation with a nice-looking, gray-haired guy in the doctor's office the other day. He told me his wife had passed away a few years earlier. Hmm, I thought, what a nice guy. He also went on to tell me of some minor health issues he was experiencing but what did one expect at his age? It turns out he was one year younger than my son. Yikes, I just can't get a break.

While you are picturing a guy fishing off the end of your dock with a baseball cap worn backwards the matchmakers are trying to set you up with a nice polite guy in a 3-piece suit. You can't be serious.

I did invite a dear long-time friend over for dinner. It was Valentines Day and I wrote him a nice note telling him how much his friendship had meant to me over the years. I made a special dinner and dessert to celebrate the occasion. After dinner we settled in to watch a little TV when he looked at his watch and said he had to be home by 8:30 since there was a movie he wanted to see. You have to be kidding... A few months went by and we were talking. I told him he had hurt my feelings by coming down and then leaving early to see a movie. With a puzzled look on his face he asked, "really, what was the movie?" You have to be kidding.

You are probably not going to find a divorcee in my age group. No, our best bet is the widower, and they are few and far between. When a woman does manage to find one, it is like the Oklahoma Land Grab. She can have a casserole at a widower's door faster than I can swat a fly. It might be helpful if the obituaries printed a picture of the surviving spouse. No one really needs to see a picture of the deceased. We need a picture of the one that is left behind. It's nice to know what's out there. Of course you might have to crash a few funerals but you do what you have to do.

When my son was in his 40s a coworker told him about the "Singles Dance." What the heck, he had just recently found himself single and decided to try this out. The theme was "Senior Prom." We both died laughing as he rummaged through the attic searching for an old sports coat. I waited up just to see how things went. I was pretty sure there would be a few laughs and I was not wrong. Seems there were 20 women to each guy and they had outlived him by a good 30 to 40 years.

"I danced with all of them," he said. "The last lady I danced with knowingly whispered in my ear, *you won't be back will you?* To which I replied, *probably not.*"

I have known women in their 80s who have found true love and spent out their last years happy with their choice. I just don't have the answers. I do believe we are better together and if the right person came along, who knows? For now, when it comes to men I will stick with catch and release. You know: catch them, enjoy them for awhile and then toss them back. Of course, I am sure there is a keeper out there somewhere but who knows?

LAST PAGE

Thank you for reading my little take on life. I hope some of it brightened your day, even for a minute. As they say, the glass is either half empty or half full; it's how you look at it. After I finished this book I went to my 60th class reunion and did a big u-turn in my life.

How can you be pushing 80, pull up 60 years of roots and find a relationship you thought you would never have?

I hope you will join me in my next adventure. If you think it's all behind you, think again. No matter where you are on life's path there can always be something new just around the next curve. You just have to grip that wheel and make the turn.

Put on those colored glasses and the most mundane chores can bring a smile to your face. If this book helped you do that it was well worth the printing.

I would like to thank Stephanie Gidley, my lakeside neighbor and friend and the author of *Getting To Paris,* for her encouragement in getting this book published. I am pretty sure it would not have happened without her constant support.

ABOUT THE AUTHOR

J udy grew up in a small riverside town
named Riverdale nestled in the middle
of Michigan. It was the 40s, a perfect
era to live through one's imagination. This
childhood gave her the ability to view life
on a whole different level.

She married her high school sweet heart,
Dale, right after graduation. They moved
ten miles down the road to the small college
community of Alma. Judy and her husband
Dale would raise three children there.

Growing up near the river had instilled a
love for water. For years she and her family
spent their summers camping at different
lakes until 1991 when they bought a cabin
on a lake about an hour from Alma. This was
a seasonal cabin, but a great place to spend
their summers, especially after Dale retired.
In 2005 Dale passed away. For the next 17
years Judy continued to spend summers at

the cabin. In 2019 she made a huge decision to leave her Alma home of 60 years and build a small home at the beloved lake. In 2021 her dream came true and she moved into her new lakeside home and resides there today.

Made in the USA
Monee, IL
15 May 2022

96452080R00098